College Admission 101

Expert Advice for the New Challenges in Admissions, Testing, Financial Aid, and More

3rd Edition

By Robert Franek
America's Leading College Expert from The Princeton Review

PrincetonReview.com

Penguin
Random
House

The Princeton Review
110 East 42nd St, 7th Floor
New York, NY 10017
Email: editorialsupport@review.com

Published in the United States by Penguin Random House LLC, New York, and in Canada by Random House of Canada, a division of Penguin Random House Ltd., Toronto.

ISBN: 978-0-593-45057-4
eBook ISBN: 978-0-593-45097-0
ISSN: 2575-6273 \

The Princeton Review is not affiliated with Princeton University.

Editors: Laura Rose and Aaron Riccio
Production Editor: Nina Mozes
Production Artist: Deborah Weber

Printed in the United States of America.

9 8 7 6 5 4 3 2 1

3rd Edition

Editorial

Rob Franek, Editor-in-Chief
David Soto, Senior Director, Data Operations
Stephen Koch, Senior Manager, Data Operations
Deborah Weber, Director of Production
Jason Ullmeyer, Production Design Manager
Jennifer Chapman, Senior Production Artist
Selena Coppock, Director of Editorial
Aaron Riccio, Senior Editor
Meave Shelton, Senior Editor
Chris Chimera, Editor
Orion McBean, Editor
Patricia Murphy, Editor
Laura Rose, Editor
Alexa Schmitt Bugler, Editorial Assistant

Penguin Random House Publishing Team

Tom Russell, VP, Publisher
Alison Stoltzfus, Senior Director, Publishing
Brett Wright, Senior Editor
Emily Hoffman, Assistant Managing Editor
Ellen Reed, Production Manager
Suzanne Lee, Designer
Eugenia Lo, Publishing Assistant

Acknowledgments

This book would not have been possible without the following individuals at The Princeton Review and beyond: Pia Aliperti, Kristen O'Toole, Emma Parker, Suzanne Podhurst, Aaron Riccio, Laura Rose, and Deborah Weber. My continued thanks to our data collection masters David Soto and Stephen Koch for their successful efforts in amassing and accurately representing the statistical data that informs parts of this book.

Most of all, thank you to my readers—I hope this book proves useful in your college searches, applications, and overall college admission journeys. Keep asking the tough questions. Good luck!

Robert Franek

Table of Contents

Author's Note ix

About the Author xi

Get More (Free) Content xii

Introduction 1

How has college admission changed since 2020? 1

Is a college degree worth the price? 6

Is online or hybrid college learning worth the price? 8

What is the "best" college? 10

Chapter 1: College Research 13

How has college life changed since 2020? 16

How do I determine the best college or university for me? 19

How important are college rankings? 31

When should I start my college research? 33

How many schools should I apply to? 34

How can I get the most out of a college visit? 36

How can I research colleges if I can't visit campus? 39

Chapter 2: Standardized Tests 43

What changes are coming to the PSAT and SAT? 45

How are SAT or ACT test scores used in the admission process
and how important are they? 47

Will colleges see my PSAT scores? 49

How is the PSAT used in determining National Merit Scholarships? 50

What does it mean when a college is "test-optional"? 51

Should I still take the ACT or SAT if I'm looking at test-optional
schools? 53

What can I do to get into a test-optional school? 54

Which test should I choose: SAT or ACT?.....................................56

Should I take BOTH the SAT and ACT? 59

When should I take the SAT or ACT?...60

If I take either test more than once, which scores will colleges see?..........61

How can I improve my standardized test scores? 63

What should I do if my SAT or ACT score wasn't great and I
can't get another testing spot?...65

Do I need to take AP exams?...67

What should I expect if I need to take an at-home exam?..........69

What's an International Baccalaureate (IB) Diploma? How do college
admissions counselors treat an IB diploma? 71

Chapter 3: High School Transcripts **75**

How do I make online learning work for me?.................................77

What should I be doing in 9th and 10th grades to prepare
for the college admission process? 79

What should I be doing in 11th and 12th grades to prepare
for the college admission process?..82

How will pass/fail or nontraditional grading affect my admission chances?..88

Is it better to have a B in an honors/AP course or an A in a
regular/easier course? 89

My school doesn't publish class rank. Will that hurt my application?.........90

What carries more weight on a college application: GPA or
test scores?..91

Which electives should I take? 92

How do college admission officers view applications from public
school students vs. those from private school students?..........................93

How do I address my high school disciplinary record on
my application?..95

Chapter 4: Extracurricular Activities **97**

How do college admissions officers view extracurricular activities
within an application?...99

What should I do if my extracurricular activities were canceled?.............101

What can student athletes do if they are temporarily unable
to play their sport? 103

Does having a job carry as much weight as school-related
extracurricular activities? 106

What sort of jobs/extracurriculars can I do remotely? 107

Chapter 5: Financial Aid & Scholarships 111

What is the FAFSA? 114

What is my Expected Family Contribution? 117

What's the CSS/Financial Aid Profile? 118

What financial information do I need to apply for financial aid
using the FAFSA and/or the CSS Profile? 119

How does the financial aid application process differ from
the admission process? 121

What is in my financial aid package? 122

What is the difference between need-based and merit-based
financial aid? 125

How do I look for scholarships? 126

How do I save/pay for college? 127

If my first-choice school's online college calculator shows that I
can't afford it, should I bother applying? 129

What is a need-blind school? 134

Will I be penalized if I apply for financial aid? Will colleges look
favorably on me if I don't apply for financial aid? 136

Can I appeal my financial aid decision? 138

Is it a smart move to attend a two year / associates degree-granting
school first to save money? 139

Chapter 6: Application 143

What is the Common Application? 145

Are there other applications like the Common Application?
Is one better than another? 147

What do admission officers look for in an application essay? ...150

How do I write a game-changing college essay? 152

When should I start the application process? 154

Should I declare a major on my application or apply undecided?............156

How important is optional or supplemental application material? 157

Is a college interview required? What should I expect?......................158

Who should I ask to write my letters of recommendation?...................161

Chapter 7: Inside the Admissions Office **165**

What are my chances of getting into my dream school? 167

How are my application materials reviewed? 169

Who is on the admission committee? 171

What is the single most important thing admission officers look
for in an application?...172

Will applying Early Decision or Early Action give me a leg up? 174

What does it mean to be deferred? What can I do to improve
my chances of acceptance?..177

What if I don't get accepted to my first-choice school?...................179

What are my chances of getting off the waitlist? 180

Do admission officers look at prospective students' social
media accounts?...181

How much weight do schools put on intangibles like "grit"?...............183

Chapter 8: Etc....**185**

Is the admission process different for international students?...............187

How difficult is transferring between colleges?...........................190

Should I take a gap year before starting college?.........................194

What if I need additional accommodations (and will requesting
them hurt my chances of admission)?...................................197

How highly should I weigh a school's stance on social and
ethical issues? 200

What impact will cheaters have on my admissions chances?................202

How can a parent participate most effectively in their child's
college application process? 204

How do I balance schoolwork, extracurriculars, test prep,
college applications, family, social life, and SANITY?!...................208

Appendix **211**

Hands down, what I love best about my job here at The Princeton Review is spending direct, quality time with college-bound students and their families. It sounds like a canned talking point, right? The head of content for a global educational services company likes working with students and their families? But, I'm not fibbing, not even a syllable. Here's why—every day you teach me how to be better at my job.

I spend most of the academic year speaking to students, parents, counselors, and educators alike. Whether I'm teaching students and parents the basics or the more advanced lessons around the college process, the most motivating part of that exchange is always the privilege of listening to each of you. Here's the logic: if I can understand your college goals along with the stuff that stresses you, confuses you, and plain-old scares you about the admissions process, then I can create the right kinds of resources to put you on the path to achieving those goals. Meeting and talking with you only reinforces my overall mission to assuage anxiety around the college admission process and create the next class of informed and fearless college seekers. Now, that's awesome, indeed!

The last several years have been more tumultuous and uncertain than ever, but though the effects of the coronavirus pandemic linger on, students and faculty alike are finding ways to press forward. This book presents the clearest answers I can provide to the most frequent, savvy, and urgent questions that I've been getting, including through our YouTube channel: concerns about remote learning, test-optional schools, and changes to standardized tests. I haven't just been reaching millions of people this year alone through TV, radio, and online sources: I've been listening, and I want to give you actionable next steps, now more than ever.

Wondering how to handle applications if your extracurriculars were canceled? How to get the most out of a college tour whether you're on the physical campus or online? Which standardized tests to take? Have nitty-gritty questions about your high school schedule? How about the financial aid process? I've got you covered for each of these key questions, and so many more. My goal, and ours at The Princeton Review, is to help you succeed in each step of your educational journey. Consider *College Admission 101* your primer to do just that.

The information in this book is up-to-date for students graduating in 2023 (and we've already got our eye on upcoming changes to the SAT in 2024), but it's also a useful guide for any student in high school, parents of high schoolers (and even middle schoolers), parents who attended college themselves, parents who didn't attend college, families new to the United States, and more. In short, no one should ever feel excluded or unprepared for the college search and application process. From SAT scores to scholarships, this book provides straightforward answers to questions about college topics and is meant for anyone and everyone interested in attending college.

Thanks to each of you for putting your faith in me and our full team at The Princeton Review. I very much hope you find this book a great resource in your college admission journey. It's been a genuine pleasure bringing it to you.

Robert Franek

About the Author

Rob Franek, Editor-in-Chief at The Princeton Review, is a nationally recognized expert on higher education and a college aficionado. He visits more than 50 colleges a year. Over his 28-year career in education, he has served as a college admissions administrator, test prep teacher, author, and lecturer. He is lead author of The Princeton Review's annual book, *The Best 388 Colleges*, as well as *The Best Value Colleges*. He is also author of *Colleges That Create Futures: 50 Schools That Launch Careers by Going Beyond the Classroom*, and co-author of *If the U Fits: Expert Advice on Finding the Right College and Getting Accepted*. Rob gives dozens of presentations a year to audiences of teachers, parents, and students on trending education and college topics. Follow his tweets at @RobFranek.

Get More
(Free) Content
at PrincetonReview.com/guidebooks

As easy as 1·2·3

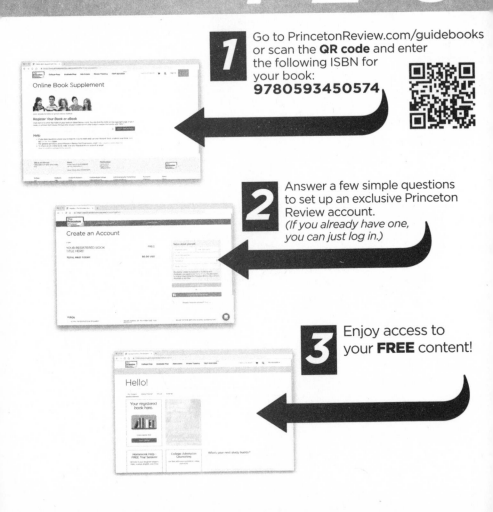

1 Go to PrincetonReview.com/guidebooks or scan the **QR code** and enter the following ISBN for your book:
9780593450574

2 Answer a few simple questions to set up an exclusive Princeton Review account.
(If you already have one, you can just log in.)

3 Enjoy access to your **FREE** content!

Once you've registered, you can...

- Take a full-length practice SAT and/or ACT

- Get valuable advice about the college application process, including tips for writing a great essay and where to apply for financial aid

- If you're still choosing between colleges, use our searchable rankings of *The Best 388 Colleges* to find out more information about your dream school

- Access the Index to this book and a variety of printable resources including: a high school testing calendar and college prep checklists

- Check to see if there have been any corrections or updates to this edition

Need to report a potential **content** issue?

 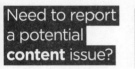

Contact **EditorialSupport@review.com** and include:

- full title of the book
- ISBN
- page number

Need to report a **technical** issue?

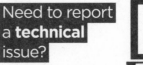 

Contact **TPRStudentTech@review.com** and provide:

- your full name
- email address used to register the book
- full book title and ISBN
- Operating system (Mac/PC) and browser (Chrome, Firefox, Safari, etc.)

Introduction

Students, you face a college admissions landscape unlike any before. The ongoing COVID-19 pandemic has radically upended the admissions process. You'll face new challenges in everything from standardized testing and grades to extracurriculars and college visits. The aim of this book is to help you navigate the college admission process and answer the essential application questions that high school students and parents ask me about on the official The Princeton Review YouTube channel, at college-bound events and webinars, and that our own college admission experts hear from clients.

Before I get into the nitty-gritty details of the college admission process, however, I want to address the big picture.

How has college admission changed since 2020?

I'd love to tell you differently, but planning, applying, and paying for college has always been an arduous and anxiety-inducing process. That hasn't really changed. Electronic options, some of which were accelerated due to the need for quarantine, have certainly made parts of the application process more convenient. When campuses closed to protect current and prospective students by social distancing, colleges presented better virtual tour options.

More notably, the actual admission landscape has shifted and continues to do so. Applications are evaluated in an increasingly holistic fashion, and *where* students apply is also changing. For instance, for medical and financial reasons, an increasing number of students have looked to stay close to home, which can have an impact on the number of applications received by city and state colleges. The extracurriculars and job opportunities available to students have also shifted, and the seismic societal shifts of the last few years may have impacted GPAs, especially if pass/fail grading was implemented.

But just as you have adapted so have colleges. As early as the summer of 2020, admission leaders—including signatories from all the Ivy League schools—had already issued the "Care Counts in Crisis"[1] response to COVID that clarified what they expected of students:

"As admission and enrollment leaders, we recognize that we and the institutions we represent send signals that can shape students' priorities and experiences throughout high school. This collective statement seeks to clarify what we value in applicants during this time of COVID-19. We are keenly aware that students across the country and the world are experiencing many uncertainties and challenges. We primarily wish to underscore our commitment to equity and to encourage in student's self-care, balance, meaningful learning, and care for others."

Folks, the very first item in the document is assurance that your application will be assessed within the context of the obstacles and challenges you have faced during the pandemic. That's good news and so is the next part: the emphasis on self-care and balance for students. These admissions leaders want you to know that you will not be disadvantaged because your school moved to pass/fail in place of letter grades or canceled your extracurriculars, or because you confronted new responsibilities at home, or had limited access to standardized tests and campus visits. You will be viewed in the context of the curriculum, academic resources, and supports available to you.

Not convinced? Both the Common Application and the Coalition for College application provide opportunities for students to describe exactly how they have been impacted by the pandemic. You are also encouraged to communicate to colleges any factors that may have affected your academic performance, like caring for a sick relative, working to supplement your family income, or having no quiet place to study.

How will that play out for your college admissions? Let's take a quick look at the factors that affect your future college admissions chances, with an emphasis on what's changed and what remains the same. Believe me, we'll go into much more detail for each topic—often an entire chapter's worth—throughout the rest of this book.

---

[1] https://mcc.gse.harvard.edu/resources-for-colleges/endorse-care-counts-in-crisis-college-admissionsdeans-respond-to-covid-19

High School GPA

For better and worse, your high school GPA remains the most important factor in college admission decisions. That said, it's treated increasingly less as *just* a number. Your advisors work tirelessly to provide meaningful data about your high school that helps to contextualize what that GPA represents. It accounts for tectonic shifts at the classroom level—shifts to hybrid learning, for example, or pass/fail grading—as well as absences from students and teachers alike. You should treat your GPA the same way—as something that helps to explain your journey, but doesn't define it. If your grades aren't where you want them to be, it is to your advantage to tell that story.

Standardized Tests

There are fewer tests available now than ever before, since SAT Subject Tests have been phased out. The way in which they are administered also continues to shift, whether by necessity, as when some tests like the AP were temporarily given remotely and online, or by intent, as with the current plans to make the SAT a computer-adaptive test by 2024.

Their impact still cannot be undersold, especially when it comes to how valuable they can be in meriting financial aid or helping to distinguish you from other applicants. But if you were unable to take these tests, or didn't get the results you were aiming for, all is not lost. Some colleges have, temporarily or permanently, adopted measures that relax their application requirements, focusing instead on a student's high school experience. (See why I said the GPA was the most important factor?) Ultimately, if you can take the SAT, ACT, or both, you should; they give you one more opportunity to shine.

Extracurricular Activities

Colleges have recalibrated how they assess the activities that students bring to the table because for many, their circumstances did change. (For instance, even if you still met with your Model United Nations team, you might not have traveled to wider competitions with them; if you're an actor or athlete, you might have had fewer chances to take to the stage or field.) Take heart: schools won't penalize you for not availing yourself of an opportunity that didn't exist. That said, you always want to be able to show that you're doing *something*, so think creatively about how to keep yourself busy.

Honors and Awards

Colleges usually consider awards and honors in making admission decisions. I know many of you are deserving of awards and honors but are missing out because programs are (or were) temporarily put on hold. Again, don't worry. Colleges truly understand.

College Essays

Friends, this is one area of your application over which you have full control. Your college essays are more important than ever! Take extra care to make an outline, write, edit, and then edit some more. Think about what makes you, *you*. You may opt to write about how the pandemic affected you, but keep in mind that a lot of other students are likely to choose that topic, as well. Make sure that whatever you write about reveals something about who you are and what you value.

College Interviews

Many colleges encourage you to interview with an admissions representative or alumnus as part of the college application process. It's another chance to show off the unique personality traits that you'll bring to college and build a personal relationship with admissions gatekeepers. Many college interviews were already taking place over Skype or Zoom, which means that you're likely readier than ever to ace your video interview.

Recommendation Letters

Recommendation letters haven't changed a lot. Your teachers want to see you succeed, and they can still help you stand apart by singing your praises and helping to develop the picture of who you are as a person. You'll learn more about how to maintain relationships with your teachers by making remote learning work for you in Chapter 3.

Demonstrated Interest

Finally, colleges take into account your demonstrated interest—all the things you've done to show that you're a good fit for their school and that you'd be likely to attend if you are accepted. You may not be able to visit in person, but you can take an online tour. You can comb through the school website. You can talk to or email current students. Convey your sincere interest in your application and any communication you have with members of the admission team. Schools are dealing with a lot of upheaval, too, so you're likely to have an advantage in the process if they know that you're as keen on them as they are on you.

The bottom line is that lots of colleges—especially those that tend to draw students from across the country and the world—are dealing with tremendous uncertainty, just like you. They are making Herculean efforts to be fair and are not penalizing students for circumstances beyond their control. Stay focused, my friends! Keep up with your studies, stay sharp with your skills, and remain optimistic for the future. Next, I want to address two questions that tend to appear on op-ed pages each fall.

Is a college degree worth the price?

The cost of a four-year degree has been increasing faster than inflation for over 30 years. Ninety-eight percent of participants in our "College Hopes and Worries" survey reported that financial aid will be necessary to pay for college in 2021. At many institutions, financial aid includes loans—so graduates often enter an uncertain job market already loaded with debt. With that in mind, is college really the path to professional success and financial stability? Is a college degree worth the cost of tuition?

My answer is an emphatic "yes!" Of course, I'm biased—I've worked in and around college admissions for over 25 years. I have seen firsthand how young people use the tools and experiences they acquire in colleges and universities to achieve their personal and professional goals. Fortunately, there is plenty of data to confirm my anecdotal observations.

In 2020, adults with a bachelor's degree saw significantly higher median earnings and a lower unemployment rate than those with only a high school diploma.

Education attained	Unemployment rate		Median weekly earnings
	2019	2020	2020
Professional degree	1.6%	3.1%	$1,893
Master's degree	2.0%	4.1%	$1,545
Bachelor's degree	2.2%	5.5%	$1,305
High school diploma only	3.7%	9.0%	$781
All workers	3.0%	6.7%	$982

Note: Data is for persons age 25 and over. Earnings are for full-time wage and salary workers. Unemployment rates were higher in 2020 than in 2019 at all education levels due to the pandemic. Source: U.S. Bureau of Labor Statistics

In fact, the Center on Education and the Workforce at Georgetown University calculates that a bachelor's degree itself is worth $2.8 million on average over a lifetime, and bachelor's degree holders earn 75 percent more than those with a high school diploma alone.[2]

According to the College Board's 2019 report "Education Pays," individuals with a college education are more likely to:

- Participate in retirement plans offered by their employers
- Receive health insurance through their employers
- Vote in elections

These are merely the quantifiable gains—you'll have many, many valuable experiences on campus or as a direct result of your college experience. (I wrote about such experiences in another book, *Colleges That Create Futures: 50 Schools That Launch Careers by Going Beyond the Classroom.*)

---

[2] https://cew.georgetown.edu/cew-reports/collegepayoff2021/#resources

Is online or hybrid college learning worth the price?

In a nutshell, YES. I'm here to tell you that not only are online and hybrid learning in college worth the price but there are also extra benefits to them. You'll have more direct interactions with faculty, who are incorporating interactive features that make classes feel less like a lecture and more like a conversation. Odds are your class materials will be presented in bite-sized pieces that work better with the average student's attention span and are coupled with opportunities to ask and answer questions and respond with video or audio assignments. Online programs also tend to be more flexible with synchronous (live) and asynchronous (pre-recorded) formats that allow you to study on your own schedule. Video conferencing tools can even help you stay better connected with your fellow classmates. And hybrid learning (a combination of face-to-face and online instruction) can give you the best of both worlds.

Hybrid learning gives you all the benefits mentioned above, along with the opportunity to experience campus life and attend some in-person classes. According to Timothy White, the chancellor of California State University, the nation's largest public university system, there are career benefits to online work, too: "That's actually sort of field training for the future workforce, because when [students] graduate, chances are going to be increasing every day that they will be working in a virtual space in the future."[3]

Since 2020, most colleges and universities have become very responsive to our ever-changing environment and students' educational needs. They have adapted to implement online and hybrid learning, including utilizing new technology and teaching methods. This changing of the traditional learning model has had some unexpected and positive benefits for you, the student. You now have more flexibility with your time and commitments and more

---

[3] https://www.usatoday.com/story/news/education/2020/06/22/coronavirus-reopening-college-fall-2020/3210719001/

choice in the *way* that you learn, and since everyone learns differently, this is a great thing! Julia Thom-Levy, vice provost for academic innovation at Cornell University, stated, "We are coming out of the pandemic with an even stronger commitment to the value of in-person instruction as an essential component to our residential academic programs but that we also have a bigger toolbox of successful teaching methods available to us now. Teachers want to use the best of both going forward and will likely blend in-person instruction with digital tools that can engage students in and out of the classroom."[4]

There are still many unknowns as to what college life will be like in the future, but here's what I do know: If there's a school you want to attend and you have the opportunity to go, then go! Go even if "going" means putting on headphones and talking to your computer camera (for now). Go even if it means deferring your acceptance and taking classes at a local community college or doing remote work and then going in-person in a year. (I give plenty of advice on taking a gap year in Chapter 8). But make plans to pursue your dreams—in whatever way feels right for you and your family. If you, like me, accept the premise that a college degree is most definitely worth the cost of tuition, then that brings us to the other big question that so many students, parents, and media commentators grapple with.

---

[4]   https://www.usnews.com/education/articles/hybrid-classes-in-college-what-to-know

What is the "best" college?

There isn't one.

It might seem silly to include a question in this book that has no answer, but this is an important point that will help put your whole college admission journey into perspective. I understand why folks ask. Given the awesome life-time benefits we know a student can obtain with a college degree, it's common to make a correlative leap: the more prestigious the alma mater, the greater the rewards for the graduate. But it's important to remember that prestige and reputation—which are often major factors in college ranking methodologies—tend to be measured with one data point: a college or university's selectivity.

According to our 2021 College Hopes and Worries survey, Harvard College was the school students most named as their "dream" college and Stanford University was the school parent respondents most named as their "dream" college for their child.

Both Harvard and Stanford enjoy an excellent reputation, provide world-class resources, and feature an impressive roster of alumni. We don't need to rely on our survey results to know they are highly desirable schools—in 2021, over 57,000 students applied for admission to Harvard, and more than 55,000 applied to Stanford. Harvard accepted just 3% of the applicant pool and Stanford accepted only 4%. Are the roughly 55,000 students who applied to Harvard and the approximately 53,000 students who applied to Stanford and did not get in doomed to failure?

Of course not! And therein lies the fatal flaw in the myth of "the best col-lege." There may not be a single best overall college, but there are absolutely schools that are the best for each and every one of those applicants, and there's a best school for you out there too.

Don't let this assumption create an enormous amount of anxiety for you and your parents by creating the impression that the choices made in high school determine, or limit, all future opportunities. You do not have to attend a highly selective school in order to pursue a meaningful and lucrative career.

Salaries and Job Satisfaction

School	Grads median starting salary*	Grads median mid-career salary*	% grads reporting high job meaning*	% applicants accepted**
Massachusetts Institute of Technology	$97,300	$167,200	51%	7%
State University of New York—Binghamton	$65,200	$120,900	43%	43%
Virginia Tech	$67,900	$121,800	48%	66%
University of Illinois at Urbana-Champaign	$68,300	$123,600	43%	60%
Arizona State University	$58,900	$106,600	52%	88%

*Data from PayScale.com College Salary Report 2021. High Job Meaning refers to the percentage of respondents who answered "very much so" or "yes" to the question, "Does your work make the world a better place?"

**Data reported to The Princeton Review by the school from fall 2020 through spring 2021

While the schools in this table vary in their selectivity, there is less variation amongst the number of graduates they produce that go on to find enjoyable, well-paid opportunities in the workforce. Moreover, you are not a statistic, so don't let numbers or acceptance rates be the only factor when choosing the school that is right for you.

The road to college is long, and students and their supporters want to be sure their hard work will pay off with a degree and experience that pave the way to a successful career. But after twenty-eight years in this business, I can assure you that college and career prep are not one-size-fits-all—there are over 3,000 four-year colleges in the United States. Thoughtful research and reflection will help you find the schools that fit you best. The Princeton Review produces a number of books that can help you narrow down the choices, including *The Best Value Colleges* and *The Best 388 Colleges.*

Applying to schools that line up with your goals and interests also helps your chances of gaining acceptance. You will likely be asked why you want to attend a particular school in a supplemental essay or interview, and "Because you're the best!" won't cut it. If you identify the specific opportunities on campus that are exciting to you, that enthusiasm will come through on your application. Admissions officers are looking for students who will be active participants in their college community.

Now that we've dispensed with the "best college" myth, I have plenty to share with you about how to set yourself up for success in high school, maximize your SAT and ACT scores, find the colleges and universities that will fit you best, and craft competitive applications.

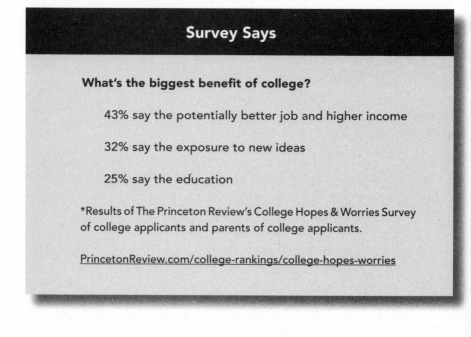

Survey Says

What's the biggest benefit of college?

43% say the potentially better job and higher income

32% say the exposure to new ideas

25% say the education

*Results of The Princeton Review's College Hopes & Worries Survey of college applicants and parents of college applicants.

PrincetonReview.com/college-rankings/college-hopes-worries

Chapter 1

College Research

How has college life changed since 2020?..16

How do I determine the best college or university for me? 19

How important are college rankings? 31

When should I start my college research?.......................................33

How many schools should I apply to? 34

How can I get the most out of a college visit?................................36

How can I research colleges if I can't visit campus?......................39

CHAPTER 1
College Research

On The Princeton Review's annual College Hopes & Worries survey, we ask nearly 14,000 high school students and their parents to answer a simple question: What would be your dream college if academic admission and cost weren't factors? Let's take a gander at the most recent results, shall we?

TOP 10 DREAM SCHOOLS	
Student Picks	Parent Picks
1. Harvard College	1. Stanford University
2. Stanford University	2. Harvard College
3. New York University	3. Princeton University
4. Columbia University	4. Massachusetts Institute of Technology
5. University of California—Los Angeles	5. Yale University
6. Princeton University	6. University of Pennsylvania
7. Massachusetts Institute of Technology	7. University of California—Los Angeles
8. University of Texas—Austin	8. New York University
9. University of Pennsylvania	9. Columbia University
10. Yale University	10. Duke University

Notice a trend? It's never been easier to get into college than it is today because there are literally 3,000 four-year colleges in the U.S. alone. But it's never been harder to get into college because we're all applying to the same small pool of schools!

The most common word I say when advising students and parents on the college selection process is "fit." Each of the colleges on the lists above is a fabulous school. While they all could be terrific fits for some students, I can guarantee you that they're not ideal fits for every student who jotted down those names on their list of dream colleges. Why? No two students are exactly alike, and no two colleges are exactly alike, either. Any college can be a dream school for the right student, and any student can find a college that will give them a stellar education and college experience.

How has college life changed since 2020?

Since 2020 and the onset of COVID-19, we have witnessed just how quickly colleges and universities will adapt to meet the needs of their students. For example, schools rapidly pivoted to online and hybrid learning. While many things about college have changed, the desire to give students the most meaningful education and experience has remained at the forefront.

As of Spring 2022, 86% of colleges were back to in-person attendance, even though a surge in omicron cases threatened to shift that. Here are some of the ways schools are seeking to adapt for the future while prioritizing your safety:

Textbooks

For both financial and physical reasons, some schools are transitioning to digital textbooks. Several schools, like Merced College, are trying the approach of renting materials to students for the semester in both formats. Grants from HEERF (the Higher Education Emergency Relief Fund) have also given some schools the opportunity to distribute free or reduced-cost materials to students who may be struggling with the financial burdens of attendance, so there are a multitude of options available for you to consider.

Many programs still have a physical option for students who prefer that medium. That said, because some tests are digital only—the SAT is joining their ranks in 2024!–it may be a good idea to at least start acclimating yourself with taking notes in a digital space.

Dining

At schools like University of Massachusetts Amherst (rated #1 for Best Campus Food in our *Best 386 Colleges*, 2021 Edition), you can expect dining halls to have fully reopened with more diverse menus than ever before. But at some colleges, like Barnard, the grab-and-go options will still remain available, so that students who may feel uncomfortable with indoor dining can still have access to nutritious meals.

Semester Structure

At the start of the pandemic, schools were looking for ways to stagger students back onto campus, potentially by spreading classes over a longer period of semesters (fall, spring, and summer) without charging additional tuition. As of now, most schools have stuck with the traditional models.

Online Learning

The biggest changes may be from the technologies that were introduced during the height of the pandemic. Remote classes and digital classrooms provided a flexibility that some students found invaluable, and those seeking to juggle their college course load with a full-time job or family obligations may want to investigate what options their school may offer.

Academic Calendar

One measure that we're still seeing at a variety of colleges, like Columbia, is a hybrid return to classrooms, even for schools that have reopened their campuses. A two-week buffer allows traveling students and faculty to quarantine, if necessary, upon returning. Other schools, like Yale University, have made more specific tweaks to their schedule, so it is essential that you confirm when your semester begins and ends, and carefully plan any travel accordingly. This too applies to vacations, as spring break may be cut from the traditional two weeks to one, if not entirely. College can be stressful, so it's important to plan when and where you'll be able to go to relax—or where you may *need* to go if on-campus housing temporarily closes.

Lectures

Expect that, even at colleges that return to fully in-person lectures, there's going to be a big push from students to maintain video recordings of those courses. Not only does this help shift the burden of keeping records from students to the schools, but it also ensures that students who miss a class for any reason are better able to catch up. Given that writing notes helps to transfer information from short-term to long-term memory, we don't recommend using this as an excuse to not note-take, though it might mean that you don't have to distractedly do so in the middle of a live course.

The important takeaway is that college and university educators care about ensuring that you have full access to your education, regardless of changing conditions or shifts in need. That said, because every college has its own resources, you'll want to make sure you list out the offerings that are most important to you, and investigate what is (and isn't) currently being offered on your campus.

How do I determine the best college or university for me?

To begin with, I always listen to how parents and students phrase this question when they approach me at the talks I give on college admission across the country. Those who ask "What is the best college or university for me?" as opposed to "What is the best college (period)?" are likely to have a more rewarding experience. After all, what may be a good choice for one person may not be the best choice for you. Here are the four main factors to consider:

- Academic fit
- Cultural fit
- Financial fit
- Career fit

All four categories are important, but certain things may be more of a priority to you. Maybe location is a top consideration—whether you want to stay close to home or go far, far away. Finances are generally a big concern for everyone, but don't just focus on the sticker price—you have more options than you think. (More on that in Chapter 5.) The most important thing to do when reading through each category is to think about what is important to *you*.

1) *Academic Fit*

This is probably the biggest of the four best-fit buckets. First and foremost, you want a school that offers the major(s) and classes that interest you. Many students have an idea of their major when they begin researching colleges, and a list of schools with strong departments in your field of choice is a great place to begin the college research process. If you're unsure of your future academic track, don't fret—you don't need to map out your entire career in your junior year in high school in order to find your best-fit colleges and universities. Read up on course descriptions and professor bios and look for topics and experiences that inspire you. Enthusiasm is key for getting the most out of your academic experience.

Class size and student/faculty ratio are just as important to keep in mind as content. Typically, schools with low student/faculty ratios see more interaction between those populations, which can allow for additional academic support during office hours, mentoring, and professional networking relationships.

Generally speaking, academics at liberal arts colleges that matriculate Bachelor of Art or Bachelor of Science degrees are often based on professor-student discussion in seminar-style classes. Larger institutions that offer a broad range of degrees and departments are likely to offer liberal arts style courses as well as larger formats: lectures, labs, and breakout sessions with teaching assistants (typically graduate students). It's important to consider what style of learning works best for you. It could be smaller classes with lots of student/faculty interaction. It might be a large seminar with minimal interaction, a combination of the two, or even some online classes that offer live or pre-recorded lectures.

Choosing a college where the courses match your learning style will set you up to succeed. To the same point, look for academic support resources you might need. Most campuses have writing centers (often dedicated specifically to first year students in required college writing courses) and peer-to-peer tutoring available to all students. If you plan to formally apply for support services, be sure to contact the academic support center on campus to review requirements, the approval process, and available resources. (You can learn more about specific services and applying for academic support in *The K&W Guide to Colleges for Students with Learning Differences* by my friends Marybeth Kravets and Imy Wax.)

Not all academic opportunities happen in the classroom, either. Go beyond department descriptions to look at any dedicated resources, opportunities to travel here or abroad, or experiential learning centers on campus (and make sure they're available to undergraduates!).

- Students at University of Alabama's College of Communication and Information Science can gain valuable professional experience at their Digital Media Center.

- In Maine, Bowdoin College owns several acres on a nearby island, home to the Schiller Coastal Studies Center, providing hands-on research tools for environmental studies and biology students.

- At Babson College in Wellesley, Massachusetts, the Center for Women's Entrepreneurial Leadership is available to undergraduate students through the CWEL Scholars program. CWEL Scholars work with "near-peer" mentors and gain professional competencies like presentation and negotiation skills.

These are just three examples—each of these schools offers tons of other opportunities, and every college and university in the country has unique resources and programs.

Does all of the above sound aggressively aspirational? Good. Aspiration is the secret sauce that helps you stay motivated and engaged through the long college application process and can help shine a spotlight on your application for admission officers. Ultimately, though, academic fit isn't based

> Go beyond the classroom to look at travel, research, and experiential learning opportunities.

solely on aspirations: eventually, you will need to look at the application data each university releases annually and compare it to your own stats. If your GPA and standardized test scores fall below the averages of the current first year class at your dream school, there are two important steps to take:

1. Expand your school list. Even if you have your heart set on a particular institution, I guarantee there is another one where you will be successful and satisfied. You can keep your eyes on your prize school while ensuring that you have more than one backup plan.

2. Make a plan to improve your grades and/or your test scores. This will be tailored to the improvements you want to make and how much time you have to make them before submitting college applications in the fall and winter of your senior year of high school. Chapters 2 and 3 of this book cover standardized tests, high school classes, and grades in detail.

Campus Wellness

College is a huge change for everyone. Yes, it's exciting, but it can also be challenging. There are new classes, new people, new living arrangements, and maybe even living in a new state. Everything is different all at once, so having the tools to cope with these changes is imperative. It's important to manage your mental, physical, and social health and well-being while in college. A resource that I highly recommend is our *College Wellness Guide*. In it, my colleague and college counselor extraordinaire Casey Rowley Barneson explains how to stay healthy and how to find services and support on campus (and beyond) for help when you need it. The book addresses many topics, including anxiety, academic stress, depression, substance abuse, healthy eating, exercise, and social connections.

2) *Cultural Fit*

"Cultural fit" can be tough to define. In this category, I include some concrete aspects of college life: institution size, demographics, location (including weather), dorms, dining services, extracurricular facilities (like the campus gym or theater) and activities (like clubs, sports, or Greek life), and events (from campus speakers to concerts). But this category can also include elements that are harder to quantify. For example, how do you feel when you're on campus or checking out the college community online? You don't have to make a vision board of your college life, but you want to be able to picture yourself feeling comfortable.

> How do you feel when you're on campus or checking out the college community online?

Start with practical matters: size and location. When I refer to campus size, I'm talking about the student population, not the acreage. The number of students on campus and the percentage of those students who will be your cohorts will influence your day-to-day experience. Student population size can also affect the size of your classes, so keep in mind what learning style works best for you. If you're considering larger schools, be sure to ask about registration and accessibility—is it easy to get the classes you want on your schedule, or competitive? This is a great question for current students—you will likely meet student representatives when you visit campus (I'll cover more about campus visits and virtual visits later in this chapter), and you can ask the admission office if they have a list of students who have volunteered to answer questions for prospective applicants.

The size of your university will also impact town-gown relations, or the overall relationship between the institution and the surrounding community, which includes your prospects for internships, part-time work, and off-campus activities. There are towns that primarily revolve around large universities, like Ann Arbor, Michigan, or Clemson, South Carolina, and there are small, rural campuses that offer a more contained experience (which students often describe as a "bubble," with both positive and negative connotations), like Colby College in Maine or Oberlin College in Ohio. Going to college in a large city where the university is just one of many influences and employers, like Philadelphia or Chicago, is a very different experience that might come with more distractions as well as a wide range of off-campus professional opportunities. You probably already have some idea about whether you'd prefer a rural or suburban campus, or how far from home you'd like to be. If you are able to have a campus visit, you can refine those preferences; what does one experience offer that the other does not? Which more closely aligns with your goals? Whether you want to go to college close to where you grew up or across the country, you will need to factor travel and/or commuting costs into your college financial planning.

Beyond these basics, think about how you want to spend your time outside of class, and look for indicators of campus social life. Do students stay on campus during the weekends? What kinds of social events does the school host? Which clubs are the most popular? Does student social life revolve around Saturday football games or quiet get-togethers, or a combination of both? If the school has fraternities and sororities, what percentage of the population goes Greek? In addition, consider what kind of atmosphere and campus culture that you would be most successful in. Do you want an atmosphere that is highly competitive or more laid back? Think about the things that matter to you, whether they be religion, the arts, Greek life, diversity, or a campus's political leanings. These are just a few suggestions and questions that can help you begin to identify what you want in a school and how to look for it. If you want to pursue any specific extracurricular activities in college, whether they made your high school resume or you want to find new opportunities, that's a great place to start. Learn if there's a campus community dedicated to your interests, and look into the accessibility of those clubs, facilities, and activities. You might even discover that there's a club you want to start on campus—if that's the case, ask about the process for setting up a club charter and available school funding for student groups. This is often the most fun part of college research.

The physical layout of a campus can also tell you a lot about how and where students socialize. First year students living on campus are often housed together and organized into smaller groups under resident advisors (RAs). RAs are there to help facilitate communal living and maintenance of shared spaces, but they may also be responsible for dorm parties and other activities that foster interaction and community-building. Outside the dorms, where do students spend time? In the library or the gym? On the quad or in the coffeehouse? All of the above? A single dining hall on campus can build a sense of unity within the student body, but it might be overwhelming for some introverted students. (Don't forget to ask about dining services, especially if you have any dietary restrictions. You'll be eating this food for four years, after all.) If most students live off campus after their first year, are there

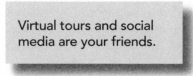

Virtual tours and social media are your friends.

student-friendly neighborhoods and businesses close to campus? What kind of transportation will you need while you're at college? Will you need a car? Public transportation? A bike? Is everything within walking distance? I am a big advocate for campus visits (more on that at the end of this chapter), but whenever a campus visit isn't a possibility, virtual tours and social media are your friends. Go beyond the official school accounts and check out any school spirit hashtags or geo-tags on campus—that way you'll see real-life posts from real students.

It's impossible to quantify every aspect of a campus social scene, and the best way to observe it is up close. Many schools offer applicants the option to stay with first or second year students in a dorm for the night and see what campus life is really like. You don't have to do this for every school where you plan to apply, but if possible, give it a go at your top choice schools. Because these visits are arranged through the admissions office, they are also a means of indicating your interest in the school to admissions officers. If interviews are a part of the admission process and are available on campus, schedule yours the day after your overnight visit. Your impressions of the campus will be fresh, so the interviewer will gain insight into what excites you about the school, and spending time on campus will give you a chance to think about what you need to know about the school to be sure it's the best fit for you. Interviewers love good questions as much as good answers.

3) *Financial Fit*

Financial fit boils down to one question: Can you afford to attend this school?

I never tell students to cross a school off their list solely because it's too expensive—there is a lot of financial aid out there ($234.9 billion total under-graduate student aid was available in 2020–21, according to the College Board's "Trends in Student Aid" report) and many different paths to pay for college. But when it comes time to commit to a college in the spring of your senior year of high school, it's important to consider cost. Keep that pricey private school on your list, but apply to a "financial safety school," too. That's a college or university that fits you academically and culturally and that you know you can afford—look at public universities, where tuition is cheaper for state residents. Other options here include living at home or with relatives while attending school, saving the cost of room and board, or attending a community college for a year or two and then transferring to your dream university for a degree.

The latter is a very affordable path to a college degree, but bear in mind that you will need to maintain stellar grades in order to be accepted as a transfer student at a competitive institution.

Parents, you will most likely bear most of the responsibility for defining "financial fit" for your student. It is very important to take a hard look at your finances, make a budget covering the tuition you can afford, and review financial aid options. I cover this in more detail in Chapter 5, and you can find detailed strategies for saving money and completing necessary forms in our book *Paying for College: Everything You Need to Maximize Financial Aid and Afford College* by my friend Kal Chany. Every school that receives federal aid is required to offer students a "calculator" that will help them project the financial aid they will receive (keep in mind that these calculators are rarely exact and may not consider talent- or merit-based aid). As I noted in my introduction, many aid packages include loans, and you can look up the average debt carried by recent graduates of every institution for a ballpark estimate on what your student will be carrying when he or she enters the job market. Some selective institutions advertise that their policy allows them to meet demonstrated student need entirely without loans—if that is the primary reason you are interested in an institution, contact the financial aid office for details early on in your application process. Even with such policies, not every student will graduate debt-free.

4) *Career Fit*

In addition to making sure the schools you're considering offer the majors and classes that interest you, find out what the college offers beyond class-room learning to ensure your career readiness. Are there opportunities for internships, co-ops, or other types of experiential learning? I also recommend visiting or contacting the career development center at each. Find out how the school supports students in preparing for the professional world: do they offer resume writing workshops? Practice interviews? Networking events with alumni? If you foresee yourself in a particular field, location, or specific workplace, ask about past students' track records of finding internships and entry-level jobs in those areas. College admission officers and career counselors are happy to highlight their institutions' success stories! If you're not sure yet which direction you'll go in, see if career coaching and personal evaluations are available for students. Lake Forest College in Illinois, for example, told us at The Princeton Review that their career services department supports "students in building their credentials in ways that will stand out to employers, and connect them with mentors and hiring professionals to grow their networks." Many institutions extend career support to alumni, too, which can be invaluable in the early post-collegiate years. As more and more students are factoring their professional plans into their college decision process, college admission and recruitment officers emphasize career support and placement when pitching their schools to prospective applicants.

Survey Says

Which college are you (or your child) most likely to choose?

41% say college that will be the best overall fit

39% say college with the best program for my (my child's) career interests

11% say college with the best academic reputation

9% say college that will be the most affordable

*Results of The Princeton Review's College Hopes & Worries Survey of college applicants and parents of college applicants.

10 College Opportunities
That Go Beyond the Classroom

Cooperative Education	Students alternate paid professional experiences with coursework. They take classes for one semester, work full-time for one semester in their co-op, and repeat. **Real campus example:** Northeastern University regularly puts students in 10,000+ co-op placements each year.
Externship Programs	Externships are temporary job-shadowing programs that last anywhere from an afternoon to a few weeks. **Real campus example:** In the spring break Externship Program, Grinnell College matches first and second years with alumni as a way to help students explore a potential career.
Internship Programs	Many schools have programs that will fund unpaid or low-paying internships, which allow students to learn more about a field or organization of interest while completing tasks or projects alongside real employees. **Real campus example:** Every year, approximately 500 students at Vassar College take on Field Work opportunities, lending their talents to nonprofits, government agencies, human services organizations, and businesses.

Leadership Training	Many colleges have dedicated leadership centers to train and mentor students in crucial skills like communication and teamwork. **Real campus example:** Undergrads at Gettysburg College can work with Leadership Coaches to apply for positions on campus and beyond. It's all part of the process to earn a Leadership Certificate from the Garthwait Leadership Center.
Projects	Projects are extended problem-solving activities that students can complete solo or in collaboration with a group, like composing a piece of music, writing a business plan, or designing a prototype. **Real campus example:** At Arizona State University, the ASU Idea Box, staffed by student entrepreneurs, is a mobile unit that travels to all ASU campuses so students can share their business plans with the community.
Research	On-campus research experiences can include working alongside your professor in a lab, writing a thesis, or completing a capstone project for your major. **Real campus example:** At Binghamton University, Summer Scholars and Artists Program fund student research and creative projects during the summer.

Service Learning	Just like it sounds, service learning combines a learning experience with community service. Students develop a greater understanding of community issues and gain skills in critical thinking and collaboration. **Real campus example:** Sharpe Community Scholars at William & Mary participate in local community projects that develop their problem-solving skills.
Student Organizations	Campus clubs unite students with shared interests and let them have fun, develop leadership skills, and gain teamwork experience. **Real campus example:** Students on the Alma College Model UN team debate current issues, earning valuable skills in public speaking and negotiation.
Unique Campus Facilities	Find the theater, lab, newsroom, or makerspace on campus that lets you build skills while doing something you love. **Real campus example:** Trinity University has professional radio and HDTV stations on campus where students produce their own content.

Study Abroad	Colleges with robust study abroad programs help facilitate academic, internship, and cultural experiences outside of the United States.
	Real campus example: Business and engineering sophomores in the University of Pittsburgh Plus3 Program can study the smartphone industry in China, car manufacturing in Germany, or coffee production in Costa Rica.

How important are college rankings?

On the one hand, I kicked off this book by telling you there's no one best college to rule them all, so you might be expecting me to say college rankings aren't very important. On the other hand, I also publish an annual *Best Colleges* book full of college ranking lists. In the words of Walt Whitman, "Do I contradict myself? Very well then I contradict myself, (I am large, I contain multitudes.)"

There are a lot of different college ranking lists available. Think of these as tools to help you find your best-fit school. A list that claims to rank schools overall is not a very precise tool. These lists are often based on the GPA and standardized test scores of enrolled students and on the school's acceptance rate. That doesn't make the #1 ranked college the best; it makes it the most competitive. And rankings that include

> It's important to understand the methodology behind any college ranking list you're using to fully understand what the ranking is telling you about the school.

things like "reputation" or "prestige" typically define those as the opinions of academics or other college presidents, not employers, hiring managers, or even current students. It's important to understand the methodology behind any ranking list you're using to fully understand what the ranking is telling you about the school. "Best value" college lists are typically based on college costs, financial aid packages, and graduate debt, and thus are perhaps more informative than ranking lists based on selectivity and reputation. If you're looking at a "best value" college ranking list, check the methodology for data points that underscore student success: retention (i.e., the percentage of students that return for sophomore year), 4-year graduation rate, and data that points to career placement or starting salary. These factors really do add up to a meaningful measurement of value.

College ranking lists in specific categories that reflect what is important to you can really help you identify your best-fit schools. The Princeton Review publishes over fifty undergraduate lists annually, most of which are based on surveys of current students—the only experts on what life is like on their campuses. We survey tens of thousands of students annually to be sure we have an accurate, up-to-date picture of life on campus. We ask students how many hours they study outside of class each week, what they think of their school administration, career services, research opportunities, study abroad programs, campus newspaper, college town, and tons more. We ask about dorms, food, political leanings, and even how happy students are (though the latter occasionally inspires some existential rumination in our open ended answers). We know which school has the top-rated radio station and theater productions, and even how much students are drinking on campus. Every year I get a few calls from administrators who are worried about where their schools landed on the rankings, but my goal is to impart information provided by real students to real applicants. You need a full and honest picture of campus life to find the schools that will best fit your goals, your learning style, and your personality.

Campus Visit Advice from a Student Who Has Been There

"Try to focus the most on what college is the best fit in terms of aligning with your future goals. Look at colleges that will allow you to explore your interests. There are thousands of hidden gems that people ignore because people focus solely on [best overall] rankings."

—College Hopes & Worries Survey

When should I start my college research?

You will want to have your final list of colleges by early fall of senior year. Making that list will require a lot of research and synthesizing information, so it's a good idea to start browsing colleges in 10th grade. Start by making a list of every college that appeals to you, and then get to work learning about each one. You may end up crossing some off quickly as you learn, for example, that they don't graduate many students in your field of interest. This early research phase will help you define your best-fit school criteria, as well. As you shape your list, look for common elements among the schools that interest you, and seek out other colleges and universities that share those qualities. If there's a college counselor at your school, ask for a meeting or video chat to discuss your interests. Your college counselor may be able to recommend schools for your list, and help identify additional support you may need to get into college, like an academic tutor, standardized test prep, or a private college coach. (Even if your counselor is not available to you until the 11th grade, starting your research early will help you find any gaps in your academic and admissions resources.) If you have a list of twenty possible schools where you'd consider applying at the end of 10th grade, you're well on your way to finding the college that fits you best. You may have a much shorter list if you had a clear idea of your "best fit" when you began your search, but there's no need to limit your options yet.

During your junior year, your top priorities should be earning stellar grades and nailing your standardized tests (Chapter 2 covers the SAT and ACT in full), but you'll need to refine that list a little. This is a good time to reach out to any current students you know and to begin visiting campuses if possible. If it's not feasible to

> As you shape your list, look for common elements among the schools that interest you.

visit a campus in person, most colleges offer virtual tours and are more than happy to connect you to student representatives or department officials who can answer your questions. By the end of junior year, you will want to have a clear idea of where you want to go, what "best fit" means to you, and whether your grades and test scores are competitive for the schools on your list.

How many schools should I apply to?

I recommend choosing somewhere between 6 to 8 schools:

- 2 dream schools (or "reach" schools)
- 2 to 4 match schools (where you'll probably, but not necessarily, be accepted)
- 2 safety schools (you and your counselor are very confident you'll be accepted and able to afford tuition)

You can adjust this number up or down as needed, but you should apply to at least one school in each category, and you don't need to apply to ten or more schools.

Survey Says

How many colleges do students apply to?

41% said they (or their child) would apply to 5 to 8 colleges

27% said they (or their child) would apply to 1 to 4 colleges

23% said they (or their child) would apply to 9 to 12 colleges

9% said they (or their child) would apply to 13 or more colleges

*Results of The Princeton Review's College Hopes & Worries Survey of college applicants and parents of college applicants.

A Crash Course in College Research

These seven sources of information have become staples for most college-bound students in their search for the right institution:

1. **College admission websites, brochures, videos, and catalogs.** You'll get a good idea of a school's academic offerings and admission requirements.

2. **Current students.** No one knows schools better than the students who attend them.

3. **College guides.** The Princeton Review's own *Best Colleges* is a great narrative guide that includes real student quotes about their colleges.

4. **College profiles.** The Princeton Review's college search tool (access it at PrincetonReview.com/college-search) offers useful information about tuition, financial aid, and more while helping students like you find and compare schools, based on specific criteria.

5. **College rankings.** Our college ranking lists cover a range of topics that applicants might be curious about such as academics, financial aid, campus amenities, and much more.

6. **College forums/discussion boards.** Unfiltered feedback from all types of sources is exciting!

7. **Your college counselor.** They will help guide your overall college search and strategize for your best application when it comes time to apply.

How can I get the most out of a college visit?

First off, *when* you visit a college matters. Look to visit the school at a point that best demonstrates the qualities that matter most to you and, ideally, at a point where students are still in class, as opposed to on break or holed up for finals. This allows you to see what the *average* day will be like for you—not just what an extreme one during Spring Fling will be. If sports or music are a big thing for you, consider going at a point where you can catch an event, or see what the school spirit is like in the lead-up to it. Do make sure, however, that you consider or ask questions about how what you're seeing may change depending on the time of year (weather, types of extracurriculars offered).

- If you're visiting schools over the summer, aim for late-August trips, when there are likely to be more students back on campus. You might also get to see athletes practicing or first-year students going through orientation activities.

- If temperatures that are too hot or cold are deal-breakers for you, try to visit a campus during its worst part of the year. Not only will this give you a sense of whether you can take the weather, but it may give you an opportunity to see how other students cope with the conditions. You might decide that college is worth a bit of seasonal discomfort.

Next, give the school an opportunity to impress you. The official campus tour—note that you may need to register to get a spot—is likely to include all of its best features, like the newly built dormitories or their rooftop planetarium. Pay attention to what you're *not* being shown and listen closely to what the other prospective students (and parents) on the tour are asking, because this will help make sure you're not overlooking anything. And make the most of your tour guide, especially if they're a current student. Do not hesitate to ask questions; the more specific the better, as this will help you to get answers that deviate from the scripted history and trivia they're reciting as they lead you around.

After the official tour, take some time to explore the campus on your own.

- Look for bulletin boards or student centers where you can get a better sense of daily and weekly on-campus activities—this is especially true if nightlife matters to you, and you want to make sure there are things to do in the evening.

- I cannot recommend highly enough that you make the library a part of your tour, as you'll likely be spending a lot of time there. If there are other services that you expect to need—like a computer lab, gym, cultural association—try to get a peek at those as well.

Outside of the tour, the school may be able to set you up with some other official experiences, and for schools that seem perfect on paper but you're not a hundred percent sure about, these opportunities can help you reach a final decision.

- If you can do an overnight program that lets you stay with a current student, do so. Eat in the cafeteria, see the late-night vibe, and make sure you like the whole package.

- Sit in on at least one lecture, ideally in a subject you care about. Class sizes may be larger and more intimidating than what you've been used to in high school, and getting a sense for the pace and scope—and level of student participation—can go a long way.

I know, I know: we've just run through a *lot* of activities to consider, and that's just at *one* college. Consider getting yourself a planner, like our *Complete College Planner*, or creating your own checklist. This will help ensure you not only have time to see and do everything you want on a campus, but by keeping a record, you can better compare the experiences when making a final decision. This will be especially useful if you schedule an interview, which I highly recommend, as it's much easier to have a meaningful, specific discussion that'll leave a positive, engaged impression with the admissions team when the school's unique features are fresh in your mind.

What questions should I be asking the college?

When you tour colleges, make sure you talk with as many current students as you can. Ask them what they love and what bothers them most about their schools. You may also want to ask:

- Are most of your classes taught by professors or teaching assistants?
- Were you able to take most of your first-choice classes?
- What is the social scene like?
- How would you describe your fellow students?

These are just a few of the many questions you will want answered. because specific questions will get you more interesting (and helpful) answers, we compiled a list of 60 great questions to ask. Check them out at PrincetonReview.com/college-advice/questions-to-ask-on-a-college-tour.

How can I research colleges if I can't visit campus?

Visiting the campuses of the colleges and universities where you are interested in studying is not required for admission but can help you learn if a college is right for you. I've got great news. You do not have to physically visit a campus to get a sense of what life is like there. After all, depending on where you live and the colleges you're considering, it may not be feasible to visit prospective colleges.

Tips for Virtual Campus Visits

Many schools offer virtual alternatives to on-campus tours on their websites or through YouVisit.com, which is a great way to get a "visual baseline" for a campus. Some schools kick it up a notch by hosting online dorm tours or providing access to residence hall floor plans. Virtual tours are great, and you can take things even further by using the Google Maps "Street View" feature as a way to explore the campus quads, the facades of libraries and laboratories, as well as parks, restaurants, and transportation options in the surrounding area.

At some schools, it may be an option to sign up to attend a virtual class in a major that interests you. Check the college's website or reach out directly to the admissions office to see what's available. Plus, schools are offering more virtual information sessions, online Q&A's with admissions deans, and live chats on social media than ever before. These offerings are opportunities to ask questions about financial aid, career services, academic support, curriculum requirements (many, though not all, schools have some general education requirements that all students must complete, regardless of major), and availability of classes, particularly for first years and/or prerequisites for more advanced courses. The admissions office at Vanderbilt University in Nashville, Tennessee, for example, sets up virtual coffee meetings so prospective students can chat with current students and faculty, and you can always keep in touch by email.

Follow your prospective school's social media accounts, but save time to dig in to non-admissions accounts too, like the Twitter for the club soccer team you'd consider joining if you enrolled or the Instagram for the very popular campus improv group. Take advantage of any connections you might have through your parents, your school counselor, or your friends to get in touch with real students who attend the colleges on your list—they are their college experts, after all. Ask them what they like—and don't like—about their school, what the workload is like, how they spend their days, and anything else that interests you.

> Schools are offering more virtual information sessions, online Q&A's with admissions deans, and live chats on social media.

What's an Information Session?

Here's what to expect:

Colleges host information sessions led by admission officers, which are great ways to learn more about schools that interest you or to find out about a school you're not yet familiar with. In the past, these have been held on campus or locally when colleges visit high schools and college fairs, but many schools now hold these virtually in webinar formats, as live videos on social media, or as pre-recorded videos hosted on their websites.

Info sessions give a broad overview of the college—the size and geographic representation of the college, popular majors, the average class size, special academic programs, and activities many of their students take advantage of.

It's the presenter's job to get the audience interested in the school. So, you'll also hear about any distinctions the college is proud of, like ranking lists they're featured on, the newly built energy efficient dorms, or how many Nobel Prize-winning professors are on campus.

While it's a good idea to bring any questions you have about the college, you're not likely to get answers to questions about your chances of admission, like, "Are my SAT scores high enough?" The presenter isn't in a position to evaluate your candidacy in that setting and will be hesitant to say anything that could later make you feel misled when you get your admissions decision.

Instead, ask questions about the admission process and the typical student the college admits. That will allow the presenter to give you the information they're comfortable sharing, like whether or not interviews are offered, the ranges of GPAs and test scores for admits, and the importance the school places on essays and letters of recommendations.

Think of a college information session like a more personal version of a brochure. You may not be able to decide whether or not the college is right for you based on the session alone. You learn more, you get questions answered by a live human being, and you get clues about whether or not you want to do even more research about the school.

Chapter 2

Standardized Tests

What changes are coming to the PSAT and SAT?..45

How are SAT or ACT test scores used in the admission process and
    how important are they?...47

Will colleges see my PSAT scores? 49

How is the PSAT used in determining National Merit Scholarships?................50

What does it mean when a college is "test-optional"?....................................51

Should I still take the ACT or SAT if I'm looking at test-optional schools?........53

What can I do to get into a test-optional school?..54

Which test should I choose: SAT or ACT? 56

Should I take BOTH the SAT and ACT?..59

When should I take the SAT or ACT? 60

If I take either test more than once, which scores will colleges see? 61

How can I improve my standardized test scores?...63

What should I do if my SAT or ACT score wasn't great and I can't get
    another testing spot?...65

Do I need to take AP exams? 67

What should I expect if I need to take an at-home exam? 69

What's an International Baccalaureate (IB) Diploma? How do college
    admission counselors treat an IB diploma? 71

CHAPTER 2
Standardized Tests

Students often ask me what tests they need to take and when. After all, there's the PSAT, AP, and IB exams, oh my! SAT and ACT scores take the lead, but college admission officers consider your performance on other standardized tests, as well. High scores can even earn you scholarship dollars. So, what happens if you didn't get to sit for a test as many times as you'd like? Or if you want to go to a "test-optional" school? I know that you have a lot of questions, so without further ado, here's my best advice on test scores and college admission.

What changes are coming to the PSAT and SAT?

For several years now, the College Board has been alluding to a digital test format, particularly after facing some security breaches with the physical exam and having to contend with the shaky reliability of pencils and papers in the age of COVID. Beginning in Fall 2023 for the PSAT and Spring 2024 for the SAT, these tests will only—setting aside those students with special accommodations—be available in a digital, adaptive format.

We at The Princeton Review are no strangers to big changes to a test: we've guided our students to success both through the 2005 and 2015 revisions, and we're prepared to do the same here. We're also well-versed in computer adaptive testing, though it's likely that you haven't yet needed to check out our graduate-level books that cover such techniques for the GRE (Graduate Record Examination) and GMAT (Graduate Management Admission Test). In short, there's no need to panic: I can assure you that our practice materials will be directly reflective of what will be on the new test well before that first new exam.

Moreover, the College Board also plans a smooth transition—it'll still be scored out of 1600, still administered at testing centers or schools, and just as predictive for college admission officers. This means that our advice in the following sections about how PSAT scores are used for the National Merit Scholarships, whether to take the SAT or ACT, and how to improve your score all stands firm. For better or worse, it also means that schools are likely to extend any test-optional policies that they adapted during COVID: Harvard's already done so for the next four years. (To be clear, some notable schools like Georgetown University will continue to require standardized scores, so make sure you do your research.)

That said, though no practice tests, questions, or digital platform examples have yet been shared by the College Board, here's what you should expect to encounter down the pike:

What does it mean to be computer adaptive?

Essentially put, students will each get an SAT that is customized to their performance. The better they do on the first section, the harder the questions they'll get for the second—but also the more points each one will be worth. (There's still no penalty for guessing, but it behooves you to answer as accurately as possible on that first section so that you can maximize your opportunities on the second.)

Will the test be getting longer?

We know that testing fatigue is a huge concern, and that it's tough to stay focused for three hours. Well, your dreams have been answered: the new version of the test will be closer to two-ish hours. That time's not only being saved by reducing all that exam setup and the time-consuming preamble from your in-person SAT monitor, but also by providing shorter reading passages and more direct questions.

Will I be able to use my calculator on the exam?

Absolutely! In fact, you'll be able to use it *more* than you're currently allowed: the "no calculator" portion of the test is being removed. And all students will have access to a built-in graphic calculator (though they can still bring their own).

There are many more questions regarding the digital SAT (and PSAT) that we don't yet have the answers for, such as whether it will address or exacerbate inequalities for student access to technology, testing security, and the predictive nature of the test. We also can't say whether more colleges will end up requiring the SAT in admissions decisions in general, for scholarship awards, or as compared to the ACT. But if you check the online student tools for this book or our YouTube channel, we'll continue to provide the answers to your questions as they come!

How are SAT or ACT scores used in the admission process and how important are they?

Colleges truly understand that these are no ordinary times. You won't be penalized for circumstances that are beyond your control. While the ACT or SAT can help you earn admission, financial aid, and academic placements, even at test-optional schools, it's true that many schools have done away with SAT/ACT admission requirements precisely because students have had to contend with extraordinary challenges—from experiencing illness to school closures to canceled test dates and test centers with limited seating capacity. Still, my advice to you: take the SAT or ACT if you can. Unless a school is "test-blind" (meaning it won't consider SAT/ACT scores), then strong SAT or ACT scores can help set you apart for both admission and financial aid.

But let's back up.

The SAT and ACT are standardized tests that are commonly used in the college admission process. The SAT is scored out of a total of 1600, and the ACT is scored out of a total of 36. The aim of both tests is to reflect students' preparedness and potential for academic success in college. Some states use either the SAT or ACT as a requirement for high school graduation. Most high school students will take one or both of these tests in 11th or 12th grade.

Why do admissions officers need a standardized test score alongside your high school grades? While grading methodology differs from one high school to the next, standardized test scores put everyone on the same scale—at least in theory. This is very much a point of debate for those of us who follow college admission trends closely. Familiarity with test-taking techniques like pacing and guessing strategies can help students raise their scores—so the SAT and ACT may not be quite the objective measurements for success that the College Board and ACT, Inc. would have us believe. Regardless, they still present an important hurdle to clear in your race to a college degree, and The Princeton Review was founded to help students clear that hurdle with ease.

The importance of SAT or ACT scores in the college application process is different at each institution of higher education. Many liberal arts schools emphasize their holistic approach to application review, which means your application is read as a story about you rather than a lab report on your education. More and more schools of all types have been reevaluating their admissions philosophies, adopting permanent or temporary test-optional policies or other accommodations for students who may be disadvantaged by lack of access to the SAT or ACT. (Don't worry, we dig more into test-optional colleges later on in this chapter). Earning high scores, however, remains a crucial part of your college admission process. There are still state university systems that have minimum score requirements or offer guaranteed acceptance for in-state applicants with scores above a certain threshold. A low test score on an otherwise stellar application will raise red flags for readers, and these scores are often used to determine merit aid eligibility—merit aid will help you pay for college without taking on debt. No matter where you apply, the three most important elements of your college application will be your test scores, your GPA, and the rigor of your high school transcript (i.e., the courses you chose to take—more on that in Chapter 3!).

Survey Says

What is the toughest part of the college admission process?

38% said taking SAT, ACT, or AP exams

31% said completing applications for admission and financial aid

20% said waiting for the decision letters; choosing which college to attend

11% said researching colleges; choosing schools to apply to

*Results of The Princeton Review's College Hopes & Worries Survey of college applicants and parents of college applicants.

Will colleges see my PSAT scores?

No, PSAT scores are not used in college admissions.

The PSAT is taken by roughly 1.6 million 11th graders each October. Your score will give you some idea of how you'll do on the SAT, which can help you form a clear plan to prep if you don't have one yet. But the PSAT isn't just a practice SAT—it will determine your eligibility for National Merit Scholarships, which can help you pay

> The PSAT isn't just a practice SAT—it will determine your eligibility for National Merit Scholarships.

for college. So you should get comfortable with the PSAT before you take it. I recommend preparing for all your standardized tests during the summer between 10th and 11th grade, before you've taken the PSAT. Why? First, prepping for the SAT and/or ACT in the summer will allow you to focus on your grades during the school year. Second, the best way to prepare for the PSAT is by preparing for the SAT itself. This will help you to use your PSAT score report to identify areas to focus on for the SAT, maximizing your study time. It will also increase your chances of scoring well enough to earn a National Merit Scholarship.

How is the PSAT used in determining National Merit Scholarships?

Students whose scores put them in the top 99th percentile of 11th grade PSAT takers for their state are recognized as National Merit Semifinalists. Historically, this percentile has included about 16,000 students. These top scorers are invited to submit their high school records, teacher recommendations, and a personal essay; many go on to win $2,500 merit scholarships while a lucky few are offered larger scholarships by colleges looking to attract students with high scores. That's pretty good motivation to prepare for the PSAT! Another 34,000 or so students who score well on the test but do not make the 99th score percentile in their states receive official letters of recognition from the National Merit Scholarship Corporation. While official recognition won't help you pay for college, it will help highlight your application inside the admissions office—especially if you follow through and score well on the SAT or ACT.

What does it mean when a college is "test-optional"?

Real talk: you can get into college even if you bomb on your standardized tests. You can get into college without ever taking a standardized test, provided you have strong grades in challenging classes and apply to one of the many accredited institutions that are test optional. Simply put, test optional means you get to decide whether you want to send SAT or ACT scores with your application. If you do, they're likely to be used for admission decisions ("optional" doesn't mean "won't consider"), as well as merit-based financial aid decisions and academic placements.

As I mentioned at the start of this chapter, whether standardized test scores truly help level the admissions playing field for students is debatable. Over the past dozen years, and especially in response to the tectonic testing disruptions caused by COVID, many selective colleges have tweaked their application processes to put less weight on SAT and ACT scores, or have made submitting them entirely optional. For some, this move is temporary. Others have made a permanent shift in their admission approach. For many schools, the choice to become test-optional aligns with their preexisting admission policies that call for a holistic view of applications and underscores the importance of best fit between student and school (which tells us that these schools are looking for something more than the highest grades and scores).

Keep in mind that schools that are newly test-optional have seen significant increases in the number of applications, making acceptance even more competitive. Often, applying without test scores requires submission of additional application materials, or meeting a specific GPA requirement. For "test-flexible" schools, applying without SAT/ACT scores requires the submission of other kinds of standardized test scores in their place, such as AP or International Baccalaureate exams. In other cases, you can apply for admission without SAT/ACT test scores, but you'll still need to submit them to be considered for merit-based financial aid.

> FairTest.org is an excellent resource for students seeking more information about test-optional schools.

If you want to apply to a school that is test-optional (especially if the policy is temporary), be sure to look at the school's policy statement to see what their stance is. For example, two schools may both be test-optional, but their websites may send very different messages. One website we looked at said the following, "The policy to remove the requirement of submitting SAT or ACT scores will allow admission officers to identify and advocate for students with a strong academic profile who may have previously been viewed as less competitive, based on their performance on a single exam." In contrast, another test-optional school stated, "We anticipate that many students who will have had reasonable and uninterrupted opportunities to take the ACT and/or SAT during 2020/2021 administrations will continue to submit results, and those results will continue to demonstrate preparation for college-level work." You should research the admission policies at your college of choice very carefully. FairTest.org is an excellent resource for students seeking more information about test-optional schools.

Should I still take the ACT or SAT if I'm looking at test-optional schools?

I strongly recommend giving at least one test a try. The more data points you present for admission teams to evaluate, the more of an opportunity you have to make yourself stand out from the crowd. SAT and ACT scores may provide that all-important distin-

> Standardized tests give you opportunities.

guishing factor for admission and merit-based aid decisions. And, since many schools still require the ACT or SAT, you won't be limiting your choices to only test-optional or test-blind schools. Having solid test scores on hand will give you a wider array of options when it comes to colleges and may be necessary for scholarship applications. The bottom line is that standardized tests give you opportunities.

Test-Optional vs. Test-Blind

Test-optional and test-blind are not the same. Test-optional schools allow you to choose whether or not to include SAT or ACT scores with your application. Test-blind schools won't look at or consider SAT or ACT scores.

What can I do to get into a test-optional school?

The University of Chicago. The University of California system. The University of Texas system. Eight, count 'em, eight Ivies. More and more colleges and universities have gone test-optional in recent years. Chances are there's at least one test-optional school on your college wish list. These admission teams still need to get a clear sense of who you are and why you'd be an amazing addition to their campus. In short, my friends, you need to do everything you can to make your application stand out.

We'll go into how to craft your college application in much more detail in Chapter 6, but here's a sneak peek. First up: research. It is critical that you be able to demonstrate to the admissions committee why you're a great fit for that school—and vice versa—and the only way to do so is to know exactly where you'd fit in with pre-existing programs. This is perhaps even more important for schools instituting some form of distance learning, as there will likely be fewer opportunities for you to figure out who you are and what you can contribute once you get there if you're not actually *there*.

So, take virtual campus tours. Follow school spirit hashtags on Twitter. Figure out what sort of programs and activities are being planned and see how you would be able to get involved with them. Search college profiles on PrincetonReview.com or grab a copy of one of our guidebooks. Once you figure out what's important to you, you can find schools that align with your goals and values. (I've got more advice on college research if you flip back to Chapter 1.)

> Do everything you can to make your application stand out.

Next, you'll want to write game-changing college essays and solicit glowing letters of recommendation (see Chapter 6). Make the most of this opportunity for the admission committee to hear directly from the source: you! Help them learn more about your character from the teachers, mentors, and coaches who have supported your growth. And finally, let me reiterate that if you can take the SAT or ACT, prep beforehand so that you can do your level best. If you achieve your score goal... fantastic! You can send your scores to schools* where they may help your application to stand out. If you don't achieve your goals, and your schools are test-optional, they never need to know. (To be clear, I emphatically recommend that you do *not* send low scores. Think about it from the college's point of view. If a school accepts a student who has reported a low score, that will be factored into the school's overall average for admission requirements, and a school that is only temporarily test-optional may not want to lower that range.)

*One quick note that for both the SAT and ACT, there is a fee to send scores after viewing them, though this fee can be dropped if you're eligible for a fee waiver.

Which test should I choose: SAT or ACT?

I hear some variation of this question a lot! SAT or ACT? Or both? Is neither an option? The vast majority of four-year colleges will accept scores from either test, and do not prefer one over the other, so it's really up to you. Most of the students we work with at The Princeton Review want guidance as to which test will allow them to get the highest score with the least amount of work. The simplest way to answer that question is to take a practice ACT and a practice SAT, including observing the standard time limits, and see how you feel and how you score. There are plenty of free or affordable ways to access practice tests online or in books (including on our website PrincetonReview.com). I typically advise students to take at least one of these exams, even if they're only applying to test-optional schools.

The SAT was redesigned in 2016 and will be updated again in 2024 to a digital-only model, so it's a different test than the one your parents remember taking. The current iteration is more similar to the ACT than ever, which makes it much easier to prep for both tests concurrently. You don't have to take *both* the SAT and ACT, but before COVID a steadily increasing number of applicants to competitive colleges were submitting scores from both tests with their applications. That's definitely a trend to watch. (Do also consider the saying "A jack of all trades; a master of none." If studying for both the SAT and ACT becomes overwhelming, it's okay to focus on just one of the two!)

Take note: there are some key differences between the two tests. There's one more reading comprehension passage on the SAT than on the ACT. The ACT uniquely has a Science section, but it tests critical thinking rather than specific science knowledge. The SAT only allows a calculator for some math questions, while the ACT allows a calculator for all math questions. And of course, the score ranges are different. A perfect score on the SAT is 1600. On the ACT, it's 36. While that's all important to know, the best way to figure out which test you'll do better on isn't to weigh all of these factors—it's to jump right in and take a couple of practice tests!

	SAT (pre-2024)	ACT
Sections	Reading Writing & Language Math	English Math Reading Science Reasoning Essay (Optional)
Time	3 hours	2 hours 55 minutes (without Essay) 3 hours 40 minutes (with Essay)
Reading Comprehension	5 passages	4 passages
Science	None	1 "science" section that really tests critical thinking, not the science you learned in school
Math	Arithmetic Algebra I & II Geometry, Trigonometry, Data Analysis *Calculator not allowed on some sections	Arithmetic Algebra I & II Geometry, Trigonometry *Calculator allowed on all sections
Essay	None	Optional (but required by some colleges). The essay prompt is designed to test how well you evaluate and analyze complex issues.
Score	400–1600	1–36
Retesting options* (see note on next page)	Entire exam	*Planned:* Entire exam OR a retest of 1, 2, or 3 sections.

Changes to Retesting Options

The ACT currently utilizes superscoring, which means that the ACT will send your highest scores from each section. This means that there's no disadvantage to retesting: your total score can only improve. (Should the ACT institute section retesting, which would allow students to specifically retake one to three sections [instead of the whole exam], this will become even truer—and easier.)

It was announced, just before the printing of this book, that the SAT would be switching to a computer-adaptive model in 2024. (Though this would still be an on-site test, as opposed to an at-home one.) The ACT is also developing its online version. Since things can quickly change, always check with both testing bodies to see if anything new is being implemented.

Should I take BOTH the SAT and ACT?

If you're one of those people who loves taking tests, and you've got the time available, this is an easy question to answer. That said, my recommendation to everyone else is very much the same. You may not like taking more tests than you need to, but admission committees have gone on the record saying that "More information is always better."

What this boils down to is that the *more* tests you take, the *more* opportunities you have—especially if schools are comparing the academic records of multiple qualified students. Unless you're applying exclusively to test-blind colleges, having both ACT and SAT scores ensures that those reviewing your application will be able to find the data they're most interested in. At selective schools in particular, a quarter or more of enrolled students submitted scores for both.

Taking both tests also gives *you* more control over what you show schools. If you only take the ACT, that's the test that you're stuck submitting. If you've taken the SAT as well, you don't have to guess which one you'd perform better on. You can make the most informed decision possible, which in turn will allow admission committees to do the same, hopefully in your favor. And if you wind up submitting good scores from both exams? You're just demonstrating academic consistency and rigor.

Beyond the application itself, test scores also often play a role in certain types of financial aid, specifically merit-based aid. These are offered both by colleges and through external programs, and the same rules mentioned above apply here. The time to realize that an ACT score would've been useful isn't once you're submitting the application and are out of testing dates.

Even if you're not planning to take both tests, at least *consider* both when you're choosing test dates. The two testing bodies have different availabilities, so if you find yourself unable to take the SAT for some reason, being prepared for the ACT as well means that you'll still be able to get satisfactory test results by your deadline.

It may seem like taking both tests is a case of overpreparing, but when it comes to your future, especially if you've got your heart set on one specific, competitive college, can one really be said to have *over*prepared?

When should I take the SAT or ACT?

Plan to take your first official sitting of either test as early as you feel comfortable and ready (from a test prep perspective). I recommend no later than the spring of 11th grade. That will leave you with plenty of time to get your scores, and if you want to raise them, plan for any targeted follow-up prep and a second official sitting. There's nothing wrong with taking the test a second time if you didn't get the scores you were hoping for at first. If you are happy with your scores, you could consider giving the other test a try, or just use 12th grade fall to focus on crafting your applications and essays.

Since 2020, both the College Board and ACT, Inc. have adapted to ensure student safety while taking the exams. Historically, both the SAT and ACT have been given 7 times a year, but there is always the possibility that a testing date will have to be canceled due to the pandemic. In order to give yourself the most opportunity, take the test as early as you feel comfortable while still allowing enough time to reschedule or retake the test if something major or unforeseen should occur. Check the official College Board and ACT websites to get the latest test date schedules.

The bottom line: both the SAT and ACT are held multiple times a year and both the College Board and ACT are making serious efforts to ensure you'll be able to take these exams in a safe way. It's possible that centers near you may have fewer seats than usual. Some states may have lower capacity and, in densely populated cities, students may have a harder time finding available seats than in less densely populated places. That's why it's important to register for the test date you're planning on as early as you can.

If I take either test more than once, which scores will colleges see?

Colleges and universities typically choose one of three options when it comes time to evaluate your standardized test scores:

- Consider all scores from all official test dates;
- Consider your highest overall score from a single test date;
- Consider a composite of your highest scores on each section from all the dates you took the test, known as a "superscore."

Each school will have its policy clearly spelled out on the institution's website and/or in your application materials. If you aren't sure which scores a school will evaluate with your application, call and ask. This will inform your test prep and test-taking strategy. It's also your responsibility to arrange for the appropriate score reports to be sent to each college from ACT, Inc. or the College Board for the SAT. It's possible that you'll apply to several schools with different test score policies.

All Scores

If you're applying to any schools that require all of your official score reports, you will want to be at the absolute top of your game each time you sit for either the SAT or ACT. Practice, practice, practice on full-length tests with the appropriate time limits as much as possible. Eliminate as many test-day variables as you possibly can: Make sure you know how to get to the test site in advance, have gas in the car and batteries in your calculator, get a good night's sleep and eat a healthy breakfast. I give this advice to all test takers, but if schools will see all your score reports, the margin for error is slim. Fortunately, fewer and fewer schools are taking this daunting approach to test scores, and if you do experience a standardized test setback, you can include a statement explaining the circumstances with your college application.

Highest Overall Score from a Single Test Date

Schools that only consider your highest overall score make the process of requesting score reports very simple, since you'll only need the one report.

Superscores

Many selective colleges use superscores, which is great for applicants, as only your best test performances count on your application. You can calculate your SAT superscore by adding your highest Math section score to your highest Evidence-Based Reading and Writing score. When you apply to a school with a superscore policy, you will need to identify the test dates on which you received your highest score on each SAT test section (Math and Evidence-Based Reading and Writing) and send in score reports from each of those dates. The admissions office will then calculate your superscore and dismiss the lesser scores. ACT, Inc. can provide an automatically calculated superscore for students who have taken the ACT more than once. ACT, Inc. takes the average of the four best subject scores (Math, Science, Reading, and English) from each ACT test attempt and counts it as your official score. (That doesn't mean that you *have* to send your superscore or that all colleges will accept it, so do your research.)

The College Board and ACT, Inc. have historically charged a small fee for each score report. Colleges are increasingly accepting self-reported scores on applications—that means you won't have to pay for each official report to be sent to each school where you are applying, but can enter scores on your application yourself. You will still need to send in an official score report to confirm your self-reported scores if you are accepted. The College Board and ACT, Inc. have also introduced more fee-waiver policies that make it easier and cheaper for students to submit official score reports with their applications.

How can I improve my standardized test scores?

Good scores don't come without putting in the work. Improving your standardized test scores boils down to identifying three things: (1) the scores you have; (2) the scores you need; and (3) a plan to close the gap. You might only get one chance to take an official administration of a particular standardized test, which means you'll want to score as well as you can to make the strongest possible case for admissions, merit-based financial aid, and academic placements.

You've heard me rhapsodize at length about the benefits of taking SAT and ACT practice tests, and I want you to know that there are practice tests available for them all. AP exams, PSAT, IB–make sure that you simulate test day conditions as closely as possible, including time limits, to get your personal baseline score from the practice test.

Next, let's consider "the scores you need." For starters, look up the college profile for each of your prospective schools on PrincetonReview.com. Go to the Admissions tab on each profile, and check the 25th through 75th percentile SAT and ACT scores of enrolled students. The scores you see toward the higher end of that range are your goals to set—and, ideally, the ones to beat. Remember: You don't have to submit scores to test-optional schools, but if you do choose to submit them, those scores *will* be considered for admission. To help your application and your financial aid prospects, they'll need to be competitive with the scores of accepted, enrolled students at the schools on your list. (More about this a few pages back in "What can I do to get into a test-optional school?") Scores can be a chance to shine.

As for AP exams, each college on your list will have its own policies about what AP score will translate to college credit, so you're aiming for the highest score possible to give you the most options. Consistently getting a 3 in practice exams shows you there is room to shake up your prep strategy.

To close the gap between the scores you have and the scores colleges require, you'll need a tool kit. I cannot recommend highly enough our own Princeton Review prep books, online courses (including ones that come with score guarantees), and tutors. But there are tons of options out there. How do you know where you need to improve? Target your prep based on your practice test performance, and drill down on the areas that presented the greatest challenges for you, like timing, content, or question types. Are there patterns? Did you tend to struggle more on algebra questions over the geometry ones? Did you take a hard, convoluted approach when there was an easier, more strategic way to answer the question? Analyzing why you got questions wrong (and right!) will help you pin down what you know and don't know, and what strategies worked and didn't work.

When prepping for standardized tests, I always recommend working when you have the availability to focus your time and energy. Keep up a consistent review schedule and continue to practice about 30 minutes a day to keep your skills sharp. Once you're fully prepared to take a standardized test, the goal is to *stay* prepared. For more tips on how to get a great test score, check out my videos on our YouTube channel (youtube.com/c/ThePrincetonReview/videos).

What should I do if my SAT or ACT score wasn't great, and I can't get another testing spot?

Take a deep breath. Know that whatever happens, you will be among an entire cohort of students in the same situation—students whose test dates have been canceled or postponed and who may not have had the opportunity to sit for these tests as many times as they would like. The College Board and ACT, Inc. understand this and college admissions teams will understand this, as well.

Here are a few additional considerations that should ease your mind:

1. **You still might be able to retake the test.** Check the ACT website to see if their standby testing option is available and the College Board website to see if waitlist registration for the SAT is available. Due to the ongoing changes with the pandemic, colleges have become more flexible and accommodating. Should opportunities to complete the requirements of college applications not be available, colleges are very likely either to change the requirements or move the deadline so that students can meet them.

2. **Are the schools on your list test-optional? You've got the leverage in this situation!** The University of California system, for one, has famously removed its SAT/ACT college admission requirement by going test-optional for fall of 2022 admission and test-blind for fall of 2023 and 2024. These UC schools are not alone! If you're applying to schools that are test-optional, taking the SAT or ACT doesn't mean you have to report your scores.

3. **You are more than your test score.** SAT/ACT scores are one piece of your college application and don't tell the full story of who you are. Your college essays, teacher recommendations, and extracurriculars all play a role in making you a multi-layered candidate. So do your coding skills, your love for piano, the way you take care of your siblings, late-night chess battles with your dad, and those epic Lego dioramas you create on the dining room table. What interests you outside of the classroom can provide fantastic fodder that will set you apart from other applicants.

So, don't give the SAT/ACT tests more or less weight than they deserve. If you are able to schedule another test date due to new college application deadlines, that's great. If not, shift your focus to the other aspects of your application that you *can* control, and take heart.

Do I need to take AP exams?

Most colleges and universities do not require Advanced Placement (AP) scores for admission—but they will make your application more competitive. AP courses are college-level classes taught in high school, usually during junior and senior year, and culminate each May/June with subject exams that are scored 1–5. AP exams are typically a combination of multiple choice and short-answer questions that run two to three hours. (Some language tests included an audio component.)

That might sound like a lot of work for a score that isn't absolutely necessary—and only out of 5! But AP courses and exams can give both you and your college application a whole lot of power. AP classes on your high school transcript show admissions officers that you're academically engaged and willing to challenge yourself—that's what I mean when I talk about the rigor of your high school transcript. (For schools that are test-optional, your ability to demonstrate such engagement will be more important than ever!) You can pursue subjects that you find compelling, and you will develop research and analytical skills that will help you succeed in college. Many colleges give course credits for AP scores of 4 or 5. Starting college with a few academic credits already in your pocket can potentially help you place out of prerequisite classes; it can free up your schedule to pursue an academic minor, an internship, or a part-time job. Several AP credits and careful academic planning can also help you graduate a semester or even a year early, which is one strategy for keeping the overall cost of your degree down. Being able to skip a class that your peers have to take may lessen the competition you'd face during registration.

As you chart your course through high school, find out what AP classes are available at your school. There are 38 subject exams, but not every subject is taught at all high schools, and you'll need to know any courses you're required to take before entering an AP course (for example, you may need to take a couple of years of honors classes in Spanish to enroll in AP Spanish your senior year). This sort of pre-planning is important because when the time comes to sign up for APs, you want to be at the front of that list.

That said, while taking challenging courses is essential to building a college-ready high school transcript, overloading your schedule in one semester or year can cause a lot of stress and set up unnecessary obstacles to achieving the best grades possible. Choose AP subjects that interest you and in which you received good grades in introductory level courses. Balance your workload by taking one or two AP classes each semester in 11th and 12th grade, rather than trying to pursue an all-AP, all-the-time schedule.

> When you take an AP class, make a plan to prep for the exam by March 1.

When you take an AP class, make a plan to prep for the exam by March 1. The course will give you a deep dive into material covered on the test, but as with all standardized tests, you will benefit from getting familiar with the test format. You'll sit for the test in early May or June, so you'll need to schedule time to review class material and work practice questions within accurate time limits (along with all your other homework, extracurriculars, test prep, and down time!). Look at your AP exams as a chance to brag to admissions officers about your knowledge of subjects that excite you.

What should I expect if I need to take an at-home exam?

An online, take-at-home version of the AP exam debuted in May 2020 in response to the impact of COVID-19. It's possible that future iterations of the AP and other exams will be held online as well. If that's the case, then you can likely expect a test experience that resembles the format below. I say, *likely*, because—here comes my refrain—things not only can change, but are changing! Double-check the official testing websites in the months leading up to your exam for the most up-to-date information.

The best way to avoid being caught off guard is to prepare for everything. (It's also a good way to overprepare if there end up being no changes.) For one, you may experience a shorter test. The at-home APs introduced in May 2020 were 45-minute, free-response tests that students could choose to take on a date in either early May or June. (By the way, free-response is the format of most college-level exams, too!)

One of the most important things to know is what the testing conditions will be for your at-home exam. Will you be able to use any type of device (tablet, laptop/desktop, or smartphone)? Can your answers be typed and electronically sent or can they be handwritten and submitted as a digital photo? Make sure you find out the specific requirements from the official testing body. If you will be taking an at-home exam, make sure that wherever you set up shop is quiet and comfortable and that you've configured everything you need—fresh batteries in your calculator! Up-to-date web browser!— in advance of test day. Practice in that environment so you are completely relaxed and prepared. If you're worried about your internet, device, or setup at home, you should reach out to your counselor or directly to the testing body.

Another thing to note: if your online exam is an open-book, open-note test, meaning you are allowed to have your textbooks and class notes by your side, let me caution you that flipping through your notes is never a good use of your time. The best way to prepare your notes is to know exactly what you have in advance and to organize it thoughtfully. That way, if you do need to look up a quick formula or fact, it will *literally* be at your fingertips.

> The best way to avoid being caught off guard is to prepare for everything.

Regardless of which online exam you are taking, you can (and should!) practice everything beforehand—from timing and the use of your notes or formula sheets to the mechanics of actually uploading and submitting your finished work. Knowing exactly what to expect is a surefire way to feel as comfortable as possible—at home or otherwise—on exam day.

What's an International Baccalaureate (IB) Diploma? How do college admissions counselors treat an IB diploma?

The International Baccalaureate Diploma Programme is another high school curriculum option that, like honors or AP classes, gives you opportunities to challenge yourself academically and signal to admissions officers that you're capable of rigorous academic work. It is a specific curriculum and set of assessments completed in the final two years of high school, and it is only available at some U.S. high schools that have been accredited by the International Baccalaureate. It was developed in Switzerland in the 1960s by an international coalition of educators, with the goal of creating a curriculum that prepares students for college-level academics that could be implemented globally. If you're a high school junior and this is the first time you're learning about the International Baccalaureate program, I don't want you to panic over a missed opportunity! Many U.S. high schools do not offer the IB program, but do offer other challenging classes and programs (like AP courses) that will give weight to your transcript. Going for an IB diploma is a decision you want to make with input from your parents and school counselor, possibly as early as 8th grade, as you will need to attend a high school that offers the program.

When students and parents ask about IB diplomas and college admissions, they're usually in one of two camps: either they're already pursuing an IB (often overseas) and are worried that U.S. colleges and universities don't recognize its qualifications, or they want to know if AP credits or IB credits are more impressive to admissions officers. I've got good news for everyone: admissions officers at U.S. schools are familiar with the International Baccalaureate and the high level of academic study and performance it entails, and most of the admissions professionals I've met rank AP credits and IB credits on a college application equally. They both reflect a student who pursues academic achievement

> Most admissions professionals rank AP credits and IB credits on a college application equally.

Some schools award college credits for IB subjects.

through the opportunities available—AP classes are more widely available to high school students in the United States than IB classes. The IB diploma may not be an option at your school, or it might not be the best curriculum for your learning style, but that won't count against you if your transcript includes honors and/or AP courses, or even specialized summer programs.

If an IB diploma is an option for you, it's a unique opportunity that you should discuss with your high school counselor or a teacher you trust to honestly evaluate your academic potential. Individual colleges and universities have different policies regarding IB credits, but as with APs, some schools award college credits for IB subjects. There are also IB-specific scholarships available at universities worldwide, including almost sixty schools in the United States.

High School Testing Timeline

Extracurricular activities, school commitments, and other factors play into when and how you're going to prepare for the SAT and ACT. Folks, there's no perfect plan, but here's what I recommend for students going into their junior year.

☐ **Summer before junior year:** Prep for the SAT and take it in August or October for the first time.

☐ **October:** Take the PSAT.

☐ **November/December:** Take the SAT one more time.

☐ **February:** Start prepping for the ACT and take it for the first time.

☐ **April:** Take the ACT one more time.

☐ **May:** Study, and take your AP tests.

☐ **Summer before senior year:** You can take the SAT or ACT one more time if necessary. If you take a summer test, you'll receive scores in time for Early Action or Early Decision deadlines.

Chapter 3

High School Transcripts

How do I make online learning work for me? 77

What should I be doing in 9th and 10th grades to prepare for the
college admission process? 79

What should I be doing in 11th and 12th grades to prepare for the
college admission process?..82

How will pass/fail or nontraditional grading affect my admission chances? 88

Is it better to have a B in an honors/AP course or an A in a
regular/easier course? 89

My school doesn't publish class rank. Will that hurt my application?...............90

What carries more weight on a college application: GPA or test scores?.........91

Which electives should I take?...92

How do college admission officers view applications from public school
students vs. those from private school students?...93

How do I address my high school disciplinary record on my application?........95

High School Transcripts

Colleges care about the classes you take every year until high school graduation. So, should you sign up for AP Calculus and AP Physics the same year? Take it easy early on, and then pile on the challenging work junior year?

The general rule is to take five solid academic subjects a year in English, math, social studies, science, and foreign language. My tips will help you choose the right high school classes each year and understand how your GPA factors into college applications.

How do I make online learning work for me?

When it comes to online learning, you can do more than just "get by." You can thrive. Whether your high school is offering some or all online classes, or you're unable to attend in-person classes for any reason, knowing how to make online learning work for you is essential.

Before we jump into class schedules and GPA, let's look at all the ways you can capitalize on the advantages of online instruction so that it benefits you.

1. **Stay organized.** It's more important than ever to put every single class and every single assignment into one big calendar. Staying on top of all your assignments is key, as you're not likely to get the same usual reminders that you'd get in person, like your classmates chatting about an upcoming problem set on the way to class. If getting organized is challenging for you, check out our *Complete Homework Planner* for useful tips and tricks to complete your assignments and stay on track.

2. **Treat your online classes with as much seriousness as you would your in-person classes.** Make sure you attend class. (This is especially true if you have any lectures that are asynchronous, meaning pre-recorded and posted online so you can watch anytime.) Arrive on time. Take notes. If the lesson is happening in real time, ask questions. Engage with the material. If class is asynchronous, put time in your schedule to regularly do the classwork, just as you would in a live, synchronous class. The habits you cultivate now will serve you well in your future educational and professional life.

3. **Automatically add any virtual office hours for your instructors to your calendar.** Virtual office hours are a time period you can "drop in" online and ask your teacher questions about the lesson, get extra help when you're stuck, or review how you're performing in the course. If your instructors are making virtual office hours available, make a habit of going regularly. If you aren't having as much face-to-face interaction these days, you'll want to ensure, first, that your instructors know you and know that you're a serious learner, and second, that you're understanding the material as you go along. Problems are much easier to address when you catch them early!

4. **Try to replicate the support systems you'd have under ordinary circumstances.** We've already talked about showing up to office hours. You can also email your instructor if you have questions. Beyond that, make sure that you are an engaged member of your class community. Create or join smaller virtual study groups. Set up online meetings to talk about the material and test each other. Keep your peer-to-peer connections strong. A huge part of your educational experience will be the relationships you cultivate with your classmates.

5. **Get into "work mode."** Folks, it's both a physical state of being and a state of mind. Set up your desk, or wherever you'll attend classes and do schoolwork, like a workstation. All the better if your workstation is in a room with a door that closes! Get dressed in the clothes you would wear if you were taking the same class at your physical high school. All of these tricks help you send signals to yourself that school—including online school—is a serious enterprise. Those cues can help you create the educational rhythms you've become accustomed to and that will help you succeed.

What should I be doing in 9th and 10th grades to prepare for the college admission process?

I love it when folks are ready to start thinking about the college admission process early! Planning ahead won't just set you up to succeed, it can also help make the process a lot less stressful. If you're reading this book in 9th or 10th grade, you are already ahead of the game.

First and foremost, aim for academic awesomeness for all four years of high school. Great grades in college prep courses are a key part of your college application and scholarship dollars for school. Simply put, that means you should put in the time and effort your schoolwork requires. Create study habits that work with your learning style and schedule. Tackle assignments that seem particularly challenging head on. That might mean that on a typical Tuesday night, you do the homework for your least favorite subject first and save your favorite subject for last. Or it might mean starting a project like an essay on Shakespeare or a science experiment early, so that you have time to ask for any help you might need and revise your work. Use these early years to identify the academic areas in which you need extra time and support, and you can set yourself up for success down the road. I know that high school is not always simple, though, and later in this chapter I share some advice on what you can do if you find that your best efforts are not getting your desired grade point average.

When it comes to choosing classes, think of your freshman year as the foundation of your high school experience. Set long-term goals for high school and break down the tasks you will need to complete and the decisions you will need to make to achieve those goals. For example, consider the course subjects you enjoy and in which you excel. Are there opportunities to take advanced-level classes in those subjects in your junior and senior years? If so, find out what prerequisite courses or grades you need in order to earn a seat in those classes.

Your first two years of high school is also a good time to try out electives and extracurricular activities. Challenging yourself academically and earning good grades are important and will show any admission committee that you are achievement-driven and willing to work hard; pursuing interests outside of your required courses will show them that you are intellectually curious and eager to engage with your community. This is vital information for admission at competitive schools, where officers look for the energy and unique traits you will bring to campus, in addition to academic excellence! I dig into electives later in this chapter, but I urge you to choose subjects that excite you, not what you think will impress an admission officer. Enthusiastic authenticity is impressive!

During your sophomore year, you may want to start some initial college research. If you have older siblings who are visiting college campuses, tag along! Browse online message boards, university websites and social media accounts, and pick up an annual guide like my *Best Colleges* book. Begin to imagine yourself on a college campus. What facilities and qualities will make you feel at home? Preliminary research can help you be efficient when you refine your list of target schools later on.

> You *don't* need to start prepping for the SAT or ACT in 9th grade.

You *don't* need to start prepping for the SAT or ACT in 9th grade. Of course, if you like practice, it won't hurt, but if you experience test anxiety, it may be a distraction from focusing on your grades. If you do want to get a jump on your prep for these tests, I recommend taking a couple of practice exams during sophomore year, to get a sense of the differences between the ACT and SAT (see Chapter 2). If earning National Merit Scholar status is important to you, plan to prep for the PSAT during the summer between sophomore and junior year. You will take the PSAT in October of your junior year.

College-Bound:
Freshman & Sophomore Year Checklist

Freshman Year

☐ Focus on your grades so you can earn placement for more rigorous courses.

☐ Practice your study skills, identify support resources available, and ask for help if you need it.

☐ Get to know your school and community! Explore clubs, sports, volunteer opportunities, and more.

Sophomore Year

☐ Continue to challenge yourself academically.

☐ Develop constructive relationships with your teachers.

☐ Get to know your school counselor.

☐ Commit to the activities that you really enjoy, and try to take on more responsibility.

Summer Before Junior Year

☐ This is the perfect time to prep for the SAT and ACT.

☐ Begin your college research.

What should I be doing in 11th and 12th grades to prepare for the college admission process?

Hopefully, you're not surprised to hear that these years are absolutely crucial for your college application! Junior and senior year of high school, you want to take tough courses, get great grades, prep for your standardized tests, choose schools to which you want to apply, and demonstrate leadership in your extracurricular activities. You also need to take care of yourself, manage your time well, and make sure you're seizing opportunities when they are available to you.

Put key dates in your calendar at the beginning of the school year to help stay on track:

Junior year
- Standardized test dates—confirm your local dates for each test:
  o PSAT (October)
  o AP exams (May)
  o SAT (varies)
  o ACT (varies)

- Midterms, finals, and any other major exam or project deadline dates that your teachers give you at the start of each term

- Webinars, virtual information sessions, and other online or in-person opportunities to meet with representatives from the colleges you are considering (spring)

- Long weekends when you might want to plan to visit colleges, if you are able to do so. Schedule time for virtual college tours, too! (spring)

Senior year
- Standardized test dates:
  o Fall of senior year is your last chance to take or retake the SAT or ACT.
  o Make sure you leave enough time to get your scores back before submitting your applications!

- AP exams (May). While you will most likely have committed to a college by the time these exams roll around, some universities will give college credit for a score of 4 or 5, which can help you fill language requirements, skip prerequisites for more advanced courses, and even save a little money if tuition is charged by credit rather than by semester.

- Deadlines for the colleges and universities where you'll be submitting applications—especially if you're applying early!

- Financial aid deadlines. The Free Application for Federal Student Aid, or FAFSA, is available on October 1st each year, and I always recommend getting that in as early as possible.

- Midterms, finals, and any other major exam or project deadline dates that your teachers give you at the start of each term; your fall grades will be super important to the admission committee.

- College interviews

You'll have plenty of other deadlines and appointments to keep as you get into each year—setting up the major guideposts early will save you a lot of angst.

Your grades should be your first priority throughout junior year. Even if you faced some struggles or missteps in your first two years of high school, buckling down junior year can make a big difference. An upward trend in your grades will show admission officers that you've matured and can overcome challenges. Colleges hold a similar worldview if your grades experienced a *drop* due to COVID. Many schools will overlook a grade's decline for the semesters disrupted by COVID, especially when previous semesters (and future ones!) show a student's consistent performance at a high level. If hard work and dedication aren't earning you the grades you want, ask your teacher if they can meet with you outside of class to review difficult material, form a study group, or find a tutor (your school may offer free tutoring programs, or look online for affordable options). Your teachers and high school counselors want you to succeed, so don't be afraid to ask for help if you need it.

You'll most likely be taking the PSAT in October of your junior year. Your score report won't be shared with any colleges, but it will give you a clear idea of how your scores compare to everyone else who took the same test and areas where you want to improve. The PSAT is also used to qualify for the National Merit Scholarship Program, which is a good reason to get some practice in before you officially take the test. National Merit Scholarship Finalist or Semi-finalist status is a great achievement to include on your application, and you may earn some scholarship dough in the process.

Junior spring is the perfect time to begin researching colleges—just don't lose your focus on your schoolwork while you plan for your future! Revisit Chapter 1 for my advice on college research and campus visits—both virtual and in-person.

By the summer before senior year, you're ready for the nitty-gritty test prep plans I cover in Chapter 2. Senior fall is your last chance to nail the SAT or ACT, which makes the summer before an excellent time to take a prep course and seek out extra practice on the sections of the test that you find most difficult.

Grades remain important—most colleges request copies of your final high school transcript, even if you've already been accepted. That said, senior spring is a great time to take a lighter course load and really enjoy your electives.

Keep your nose to the grindstone in the fall of your senior year—even if your GPA kicks butt and you can check standardized tests off your to-do list, you'll need time to complete your applications and proofread them thoroughly. I break down each part of the application in Chapter 6, but the best advice for applications can't be repeated enough! Start early, do a little bit at a time, and proofread, proofread, proofread!

How to Get Better Grades

One bad test, month, or quarter doesn't have to sink your GPA. You can still end up where you want to be—if you take action now!

1. **Think of class like an opportunity to study.** Take great notes, pay attention, and ask questions. That in-class study time sure adds up!

2. **Start studying before you need to.** For big assignments, start small. Stay motivated by completing a small piece of the project every few days.

3. **Get rid of homework distractions.** Even a 3-second interruption (like the time it takes to glance down at your buzzing phone) has the power to derail the task you're working on.

4. **Use your old tests and quizzes to help you study.** It's also a good idea to look over your notes every night to make sure that you've got it.

5. **Ask for help when you need it.** Students who are willing to ask for a little help impress teachers, counselors, and colleges alike. Chat with your teachers during office hours, learn about any academic resources your school offers, or try a tutor.

6. **If you can teach it, you know it.** Get to the point that you're comfortable enough with the material that you can teach it to someone else.

College-Bound:
Junior & Senior Year Checklist

Junior Year

☐ Take the SAT and ACT when you're ready.

☐ Balance schoolwork and outside-school interests.

☐ Take the most challenging courses available to you.

☐ Take the PSAT/NMSQT in October to qualify for a National Merit Scholarship and other scholarship opportunities.

☐ Start gathering teacher recommendations.

☐ Narrow your college list and make virtual campus visits.

☐ Make a plan to prepare for AP exams in May.

☐ Learn about financial aid and available scholarships.

Summer Before Senior Year

☐ Start working on your application and prewriting college essays—they take longer than you think!

☐ Make a calendar of all your application deadlines so you can stay on track.

☐ If possible, consider visiting colleges that are on the top of your target list.

☐ If you are applying for Early Decision, you should take the SAT or ACT no later than September.

Senior Fall

☐ Apply early if you're a strong candidate.

☐ Wrap up your applications and stay on top of deadlines for apps, scholarships, and financial aid.

☐ Don't get senioritis! Senior grades matter—your first term grades will definitely be used in the admissions process.

☐ Complete your last SAT/ACT by December at the latest.

Senior Spring

☐ If you still have AP exams to take, study!

☐ Send thank-you notes to your recommenders.

☐ Get ready to celebrate! Spring is all about acceptance letters rolling in.

☐ Talk to friends, family, and counselors before making your final choice.

☐ Once you decide, don't look back! Read through your college's course catalog, and look forward to the next four years.

How will pass/fail or nontraditional grading affect my admission chances?

Colleges recognize that not all high schools use the same evaluation process. Some schools measure GPA out of 5.0 or 12.0, for some schools AP and honors are the same courses, and some students get written reports instead of letter grades. So, how will you compare to applicants from "regular" schools? High school administrators and faculty, too, recognize that the quirks of their curriculum may need to be translated to college admission offices. Particularly for different GPA scales or grading systems, your high school probably has an alternative GPA formula in place, or in the case of non-letter or pass/fail grades, a formal statement explaining how students demonstrate they meet academic benchmarks. Your high school counselor, or a teacher with experience writing recommendations, should be in a position to explain to you how any questions or discrepancies have been addressed by past applicants.

And regarding any changes to the grading system because of the pandemic, colleges get it! Here's what Boston University wants prospective students to know about grades: "We understand that high schools have adopted a wide variety of policies around academic assessment and we plan to be flexible and to honor whatever decisions your school has made about grading and course requirements. Please rest assured that you will not be disadvantaged during the admissions process."[5] As another example, Union College in Schenectady, New York urges students to see these changes in grading policies as an opportunity. "This can help turn attention to some of the other things that you have done during high school, of which you are particularly proud."[6]

> "Please rest assured that you will not be disadvantaged during the admissions process."
> —Boston University

One thing to note: Pass/fail courses do not factor into your GPA. So, if your high school went pass/fail for part of the year and is now going back to a 4.0 grade point system, you'll want to do your level best in those courses.

---

[5] https://www.bu.edu/admissions/covid-19-faqs/
[6] https://www.forbes.com/sites/brennanbarnard/2020/05/07/we-get-it-college-admission-deans-speak-out

Is it better to have a B in an honors/AP course or an A in a regular/easier course?

This question is a favorite among parents! I can understand why. Most likely, you know the average test scores and GPA of the most recent incoming class at your dream school (this is information schools publish each year and report to many publishers of college rankings). But those averages don't offer much insight into the courses in which accepted students earned those grades.

I know that reducing college admission to a handful of statistics is appealing. It seems to remove the mystery from the process—but I've mentioned that most admission officers tell me that they read applications holistically. That means they don't just look at a student's stats, they look at a full secondary school transcript, including grade trends over time and the difficulty of a student's classes (alongside all of your other application materials, of course!). When The Princeton Review collected school information for our book *The Best 387 Colleges*, nearly 90% of those schools reported that both an applicant's GPA and the rigor of his or her high school transcript are very important factors in their admissions decisions.

My advice: Take the most challenging courses available to you, and work hard to earn solid grades. It will show admission committees that you are intellectually curious, up for a challenge, and willing to work hard.

All that said, I know that at the same time you're studying for those awesome grades, you're probably also preparing for standardized tests, participating in extracurricular activities, perhaps captaining a varsity team or working an after-school job, plus finding time to spend with your family and friends. It's important to avoid burning out—take it from me, stress is not a key ingredient for success! Make sure that you take some down time each week, and ask for the help you need from teachers, advisors, parents, and tutors. I want you to challenge yourself, not torture yourself!

My school doesn't publish class rank. Will that hurt my application?

I've got good news for you here! Lots of high schools are ditching class rank, and in response, many colleges and universities are making adjustments to the way they view admission factors. While class rank may help provide useful context for your high school transcript to admission officers, it doesn't really fit in with the holistic application review process that most counselors describe. You're not just a number, you're an individual with a unique set of personality traits and experiences to contribute to a campus community. The folks in admissions departments know that, and many of them will look at your application that way.

> You're not just a number, you're an individual with a unique set of personality traits and experiences to contribute to a campus community. The folks in admissions departments know that, and many of them will look at your application that way.

One important note about class rank: If you are applying to a school within a state university system, I strongly encourage you to double-check the specific school's admission practices. Class rank remains an important factor in Texas, for example, where state law offers eligible students in the top 10% of their high school class automatic admission to schools in the state university system.[7] Typically, these systems have policies in place for evaluating applicants from high schools that do not publish class rank.

---

[7] https://admissions.utexas.edu/apply/decisions

What carries more weight on a college application: GPA or test scores?

Your GPA and the rigor of your high school courses are without a doubt the most important factors on your application—but test scores run a close third. Over 70% of the colleges and universities we survey for *Best Colleges* report that standardized test scores are "important" or "very important" in their evaluation of applicants.

What does that mean for you? Practice and prep! Taking a free practice SAT or ACT will help you figure out which test is best for you and help you identify the areas in which you might want to put in a little extra effort to get the score you want. You can find the average standardized test scores of the most recently admitted class at your dream schools online, which will help you set your goal score.

Build time into your schedule to prepare for whichever test you choose, and find prep tools that fit your needs and schedule. There are many test prep options available to suit a wide range of learning styles and student schedules at a variety of prices. I'm a longtime test prep teacher for The Princeton Review. There are over 4,000 teachers and tutors here! Whether it's a book, online/classroom course or one-on-one tutoring, choose the option that's best for you. Your high school or public library may offer free or discounted resources, and your high school counselor can offer recommendations, as well.

As I mentioned in Chapter 2, some schools are test optional, which means they will consider your test scores if you submit them, but your scores are not required for you to be considered for admission. If your first choice college is test optional, you may still want to consider preparing for and taking the SAT or ACT—these scores are often important when you're applying for scholarships.

Which electives should I take?

For many pages now, I've been telling you what you should do and what you need to do to craft a competitive college application, but I'm going to stop here. Take whatever electives look interesting to you. Electives give you opportunities to explore new subjects and skills, and having a clear sense of your strengths and weaknesses will help you succeed in college and your career. If you're invested in the subject at hand, it will be less stressful to earn good grades in that subject. Your academic grades will receive closer scrutiny inside college admission offices than your elective grades, but obviously they will still factor into your overall GPA.

My one recommendation when choosing electives is that you stick with at least one or two subjects for more than one semester—chances are, electives are offered at introductory and more advanced levels at your high school. Sticking with a subject through ascending levels will show admissions officers that you're capable of making an authentic commitment and that you actively pursue subjects that interest you.

That doesn't mean that you're committed for four years to all the electives you choose in 9th grade. Taking a variety of introductory electives will expose you to new interests and talents, whether you prefer studio art, software development, or journalism. Then move on to intermediate and advanced courses in the elective subjects that you most enjoy. If you are facing a particularly challenging semester with a heavy academic course load and preparing for standardized tests on the horizon, you might consider a less intensive elective during that time. Time management is essential to maintain good grades.

How do college admission officers view applications from public school students vs. those from private school students?

All colleges accept and enroll students from both public and private schools every year.

School	% of first-year students enrolled in fall 2020 from public high schools*
Boston University	65%
George Washington University	70%
Harvard College	63%
Ohio State University Columbus	84%
Stanford University	61%
Syracuse University	65%
University of Arizona	99%
University of California Los Angeles	75%
University of Colorado Boulder	84%
University of Pennsylvania	60%
University of Virginia	73%

Data reported to The Princeton Review by the school from fall 2020 through spring 2021

Admissions officers understand that the range of resources on offer to students varies wildly from one high school to the next, whether you attend a public high school in suburban Texas, a charter school in downtown Chicago, a boarding school in Connecticut, or you're homeschooled in Oregon. Part of the work of college admissions, recruitment, and enrollment includes evaluating an application in the context of the student's academic environment. It's up to you, the applicant, to take advantage of the opportunities at hand, both for your own enrichment and to help you represent your best self on your college applications.

Private high schools do typically offer a rich variety of academics, electives, and extracurricular activities; and favorable student-teacher and student-counselor ratios. For students, that means many options for experiences and accomplishments that will make for strong college applications, and lots of institutional support for pursuing those opportunities and crafting those applications. If this sounds like your high school experience, count yourself lucky.

If you attend a public high school, you're in the vast majority of college applicants, and you have many different paths to college acceptance regardless of the resources immediately available in your school. Admissions officers are not looking for a laundry list of achievements any more than they're looking for a set of sterile statistics. They're looking at how all the elements of an application come together to show the maturity, self-reliance, and character of the student behind the application.

How do I address my high school disciplinary record on my application?

If you have any significant disciplinary or legal issues on your high school record—think suspension, not detention—you should acknowledge it in your college application. Transparency here will show that you are responsible and mature, and if you try to hide past infractions from admissions officers only to have them turn up on your high school transcript, you're only doing yourself a disservice.

> Avoid making excuses or sounding defensive, and focus on what has changed since that incident.

You will most likely have an opportunity to explain yourself in writing within your primary essay or any supporting questions on the school's application, or you may choose to speak to it in your college interview (or both). Avoid making excuses or sounding defensive, and focus on what has changed since that incident. How have you grown? What did you learn from the experience? (Spoiler: "I learned not to get caught" is not a strong message to go with here.) Don't think of any blemishes on your record as liabilities—look at them as opportunities to show your maturity and capacity for learning from mistakes.

Whether you plan to write or speak about any issues in your past, you will need a few practice rounds. You should get feedback from someone you trust on any college essay—I go into more depth on admission essays in Chapter 6—but I strongly recommend working with your school counselor on the best context for disciplinary issues on your application. Write a couple of drafts, and go over talking points with your counselor to get prepped for your admissions interview (even if interviews are optional for admission to your dream school, this is a case where making a personal connection can really help you). In exceptional cases, a college might contact your school for more details, so you want to be sure that you and your counselor are aligned on the circumstances and outcome of any disciplinary action. This advice also applies if you want to address inconsistent grades.

Chapter 4

Extracurricular Activities

How do college admissions officers view extracurricular activities within
an application? 99

What should I do if my extracurricular activities were canceled?....................101

What can student athletes do if they are temporarily unable
to play their sport?..103

Does having a job carry as much weight as school-related extracurricular
activities?..106

What sort of jobs/extracurriculars can I do remotely?....................................107

CHAPTER 4
Extracurricular Activities

I know you want to impress colleges with your accomplishments in the classroom, but your academics aren't the full picture of who you really are. Yes, colleges want bright students. But even more, they want bright, well-rounded students. That's where your extracurricular activities come in. Admissions officers are looking to create a class made up of students with diverse interests and backgrounds. They'll look closely at your extracurriculars to get a sense of the person you are and what you care about.

Of course, just like in-person classes, many extracurricular activities have been canceled across the country out of necessary health and safety precautions—which colleges understand! This chapter digs into how admission officers evaluate extracurriculars within an application.

How do college admissions officers view extracurricular activities within an application?

The core of your college application is comprised of your GPA, your standardized test scores, and your high school transcript. Taken together, these two statistics and one list of courses convey your capacity for seeking out and conquering academic chal-

> Find and commit to the extracurricular activities that you find meaningful.

lenges. But they don't say very much about your personality or non-academic interests (though this may come through in your choice of electives, depending on what is available at your high school). That's what admissions officers look for in your list of extracurricular activities. You want that list to show that you are engaged with the world outside the classroom, and that you are able to articulate how you spend your time.

Extracurricular activities on your college application include any school-affiliated, non-academic activity, like sports, clubs, or performances. You can also include any organized activities you do outside of school, like music lessons, community service, or participating in a youth group. Seasonal and part-time jobs count, too. Your list of activities may show that you're well rounded and have a range of interests. Admissions officers will also be looking for consistency and leadership. If you can keep at least one activity, sport, or job from 10th grade through graduation, you'll show that you are committed to the pursuits and people that are important to you. Taking a leadership position or otherwise demonstrating that your responsibilities progressively increased over the course of your job or involvement with an activity or community is one of the best things you can do to show maturity and accountability on your college application.

So, what extracurriculars do colleges view most favorably? I suspect that you'd have a hard time getting a single list of "ideal" college activities from any college admission officer—imagine how boring the world would be if everyone who attended college did exactly the same extracurricular activities! Plus, if you force yourself to pursue something you don't genuinely enjoy, you're less likely to stick with it, to take on additional responsibilities pertaining to it, or write a compelling college essay about it. The first rule of choosing an extracurricular that a college will view favorably is that YOU view it favorably.

Find and commit to the extracurricular activities that you find meaningful, and look at your extracurricular list like an admissions officer would once you're crafting your application. Maybe your primary extracurricular activity began with school requirements, like sports or community service, and led to more significant, long-term participation. Describing how you went from obligated to excited about a particular activity is a great story for a short application essay (when required) or an admissions interview. If the sport or activity that inspires you isn't offered at your school, you can seek out external resources, like community center classes or club sports. Taking this initiative will provide you with examples of your independence, ambition, and time management skills.

Setting yourself up for a strong college application does take some planning, but it's best to begin with what matters to you, not to a theoretical future admissions panel. By staying engaged with academics and extracurriculars, you're providing yourself with opportunities for personal growth and self-awareness—qualities that appeal to colleges.

What should I do if my extracurricular activities were canceled?

There are many reasons why extracurricular activities are canceled, anything from an absent faculty advisor to a shortage of funding to a global pandemic. It is disappointing on a number of levels if your extracurriculars are canceled. Hopefully, you enjoyed the activity, so you are probably missing it and the social engagement it provided. In addition, you may have been counting on your extracurriculars to round out your high school resume on your college applications. You may not be able to bring back the canceled activity, but here's what you *can* do.

You can continue practicing the violin even if the school orchestra is temporarily on pause. You can keep practicing your lay-up on a backyard basketball hoop even if you're not playing in any official games. You can keep working on your poetry even if your school isn't putting out the Lit Journal this year. Do what you can to keep your skills sharp. Find ways to further your passions on your own initiative, apart from a school-sanctioned setting. The admission office at MIT puts it this way: "Your specific activities were *never* what made a difference in our (admission) process—who you are, your approach to life and the world around you, and your match with MIT have always been most important."[8]

Consider it from an admission counselor's perspective. Playing on your high school basketball team conveys more than your love for the game, the way you write for your school newspaper conveys more than your passion for the written word, and even the way you hold down a regular babysitting gig conveys more than your interest in earning money. Playing a sport shows that you understand strategic thinking, determination, and healthy competition. Pursuing a creative, intellectual, or technical project shows that you're curious and motivated. Maintaining a part-time job demonstrates responsibility, a sense of professionalism, and entrepreneurial motivation. Any combination of these qualities makes for a competitive college applicant—and a contributing campus citizen.

---

[8] https://mitadmissions.org/blogs/entry/to-our-prospective-students-and-their-families/

Regardless of why your extracurricular activities were canceled, admissions officers are looking to see how you handled that challenge. Were you able to pivot in a different direction or chart a new path for yourself? You will give them a fuller picture of who you are if you can demonstrate how you coped or got creative.

I'll end with (more) wise words from the good folks at MIT, "We certainly understand (and empathize with) students who are disappointed that their activities have been disrupted by the pandemic. However, we also want to make sure that you understand there is no formula for being admitted to MIT: no magic set of clubs, sports, leadership roles, activities, or accomplishments that, of their own, get you in or keep you out." The thing with uncharted territory? There is no trodden path. Admissions officers are looking for students who can make a new way.

Straight from the Admissions Office

"We know what you had planned. We know what you already participated in and what you have accomplished. We'll do what we do every year— we'll make assumptions and inferences, which always (and I use that word intentionally) lean toward benefiting you."[9]

—Rick Clark, Director of Undergraduate Admissions at Georgia Tech

[9] https://sites.gatech.edu/admission-blog/page/3/

What can student athletes do if they are temporarily unable to play their sport?

Athletics involve competitions that require students to be able to travel, gather in a given location, and be physically able to play once there. You may find yourself unable to play your sport due to your health, new safety protocols, or even lack of funding. But the absence of valuable playing time doesn't mean that you should give up! In fact, the story of how you persevered may become a compelling part of your college story. With fewer opportunities to impress college coaches, however, you will need to get more proactive.

If you can't play because of *external* concerns—like closures or cancellations—here are some things you can do. To begin with, stay fit mentally and physically. If a coach isn't available, talk to your school counselor. These advisors can help you deal with any stress or anxiety you may feel. If you can't get footage on the field, film your workouts or training sessions and make your own skills reel to complement any game tapes you do have.

If you can't play because of an *internal* issue like an injury, keep in touch with your coach to see if there are ways for you to still be involved with the team, whether that's participating in reduced, lower-impact trainings or reviewing game footage to look for ways to help your teammates improve. Visualize the techniques and strategies you would be doing on the field so that once you've recovered, you can more readily get back into the game.

In either case, the goal is to make sure you are staying active both mentally *and* physically, on *and* off the field. You can use this time to prioritize prep for the SAT/ACT. While many colleges have gone test-optional (as we discussed in Chapter 3), student athletes will still likely have to meet academic eligibility criteria to play a sport in college, which normally includes hitting a minimum SAT/ACT score. As always, check with the individual school to see their requirements.

If you can't show your interest and ability in the sport itself, double-down on your efforts to demonstrate them directly to the athletics departments of the schools that interest you most. (This doesn't have to be in-person!) Your fundamental athletic ability matters, but coaches in particular understand the nature of injuries and cancellations, and finding ways to creatively showcase your personality, interests, and dedication as an athlete can play a vital role in setting you apart.

Do not assume that a school is not interested in you merely because you have not been approached by a scout during the year. Get your coach to write letters to the schools you are interested in. Don't sell yourself short, either. As my pal Kal Chany writes in *Paying for College*, "An average football player might not get a scholarship at Notre Dame, but the same applicant at Columbia might get a preferential package...Remember, too, that football is not the only sport in college. Schools also [seek] swimmers, tennis players, long-distance runners, and the like."

There's an old saying, "Every problem is an opportunity in disguise." You wouldn't miss an opening on the field, so don't miss this chance to focus on what makes you YOU (beyond sports). Stay sharp. Keep in shape. Remain optimistic. The right college is out there.

10 Smart Summer Activities

1. **Sharpen your study skills.** You want to start the year off strong in the fall—whether you're physically in school or learning remotely.

2. **Take an online class.** Find a class that is not available at your high school in a subject that interests you. Or take a more advanced class in a subject that you have studied.

3. **Work on your college essays.** Inspiration is important, but there's no substitute for time. Start early, sit with it, rework it, and sit with it some more.

4. **Get a job.** Your work history demonstrates your initiative and responsibility, which impresses colleges.

5. **Create your own project.** Turn your interests and talents into a summer-long project, such as practicing creative writing and submitting your work to journals that publish the work of high school students.

6. **Become an entrepreneur.** Start a business with friends that offers a service to your community.

7. **Volunteer locally.** Commit to volunteering for a few hours a week; start now and continue through your senior year.

8. **Find a research opportunity.** Use a platform like Zooniverse to contribute to scientific research or transcribe historical documents.

9. **Start your test prep.** Keep your brain in tip-top shape by picking up a prep book, taking an online course, or finding a tutor to help you manage your time.

10. **Visit colleges—either virtually or in person.** Demonstrate interest in the schools on your list by taking virtual campus tours from the comfort of your couch, or, if you are able, by physically visiting schools.

Does having a job carry as much weight as school-related extracurricular activities?

Absolutely! On a college application, an after-school job conveys that you are responsible and rise to challenges. Your classes and grades should always come first, and if you're considering applying for a job while in high school, you should feel comfortable with the amount of time and flexibility you have for your homework. If an employer is willing to ask a high school student to sacrifice school or study time for work, they probably shouldn't hire high school students. If you're already managing a challenging school/work schedule, you've taken on a great deal of responsibility, and I'd encourage you to address any time management issues with your high school counselor.

Working part-time while in high school might sometimes feel like you're missing out on both extracurricular opportunities and fun, but it's incredibly valuable for your future—in college and beyond. It might not always feel like much when you're stacking boxes or serving coffee, but each work experience leads to the next, so congratulations on entering the working world a little ahead of your peers. No matter what you do for work, there's a way to frame it strategically on your college application. For your essays and interviews, cherry-pick examples from your work experience to demonstrate that you are accountable to yourself and others, capable of constructive collaboration, and have developed your communication skills. Highlight moments of accomplishment and take pride in your work (even if you'd rather be doing something else during most of your shift).

If you hold a job in high school due to financial necessity, don't be afraid to make that clear on your application. Your experience can help you demonstrate how you handle obstacles, course-correct when work or schedules don't go as planned, and accept responsibility. Admissions officers know as well as you do that tuition is expensive, so working to earn money for tuition shows them how motivated you are to pursue higher education.

What sort of jobs/extracurriculars can I do remotely?

I have good news for you. More than a few remote work and extracurricular opportunities have cropped up during this time that you can take part in from home. As always, you'll have to follow the guidelines where you live, and of course be true to your comfort level and that of your parents, as well. Don't be afraid to be creative with your extracurricular choices! A little out of the box thinking will serve you well on college applications. Let's jump in, starting with volunteer work:

Volunteer Experience

First stop: check out Zooniverse, an online portal of important, interesting science research projects—all looking for volunteers. The nice thing about Zooniverse is that you don't need any specialized training or background to participate, and the work you do has real-world impact across many fields. If you volunteer for the "Penguin Watch" project, for example, you'll examine aerial photos of penguins from remote areas and help researchers understand why penguin populations in some regions are in decline.

Here are a few more great sites for engaging in service that helps others:
- All for Good
- American Red Cross
- Catchafire
- Crisis Text Line
- Points of Light
- Project Gutenberg
- Smithsonian Transcription Center
- Translators without Borders
- United Nations Volunteers
- World Family Children Foundation

Jobs

If you're looking for a paid gig you can do online, there are a number of places that offer opportunities. Working in customer service, for example, can often be done from home (some companies will hire you even if you're under 18). You may be able to tutor kids online. You could help teach kids a sport, especially one that doesn't require close contact, like tennis. If you're artistic or musically inclined, you could give lessons over video chat.

In fact, the sky's the limit when it comes to flexing your entrepreneurial skills. Starting your own business (or engaging with existing online e-commerce platforms for crafts and services) can showcase your talents and your initiative. Sites like Etsy and CafePress are great ways to earn money by creating art or graphic designs and selling them to others. Service-based sites like Fiverr and Upwork can help you match your skills (from coding and copywriting to data entry and design) to a range of projects or one-off professional opportunities. You could also consider letting folks in your community know that you're available to assemble furniture, mow lawns or garden, take photos, make calls (personal-assistant work), or do any number of hands-on activities that usually don't require close contact with other people.

More Ideas for Extracurriculars

As for extracurriculars, some are more conducive than others to physical distancing. Plus, you may need to take a more "self-guided" approach.

- If you're athletic (or want to be!), online classes are available for every skill level in a variety of disciplines: yoga, ballet, hip-hop, martial arts, and more. Running is also a great sport that you can do on your own—and any form of exercise is a great way to offset the stress of the admissions process, create a routine, and challenge yourself.

- If you're a musician, you can still practice every day, take online music lessons, and even perform on Facebook Live.

- If you're a writer, you can write from, well, anywhere, and submit your work to journals that publish high school students.

- If you're a future Broadway actor, you can rehearse even when you're not performing on an actual stage. Many professional auditions are now virtual, so it's worth your time to work on those monologues, practice filming yourself, and get comfortable with the process of submitting an audition tape. And if you have any recordings of your performances, create a reel!

- If you're an artist, you can still meet online with the Art Club to share and critique work for your portfolio (turn to Chapter 6 where I discuss optional or supplementary college application material) or organize a delivery of illustrations and photography to brighten up your local hospital.

- If you're a literature-lover, you can start or join a virtual book club.

- Do you enjoy speaking Spanish? You can take part in an online conversation exchange that pairs you with a native Spanish speaker who is studying English. Spend 10 minutes chatting in one language and then switch to the other.

- You can also try something brand new, like learning to code with a community like Code Academy or taking an online course through Coursera or Edx.

The point I'm making here, folks, is that while both your age and our current pandemic moment are limitations, you still have plenty of opportunities to sharpen your skills, gain meaningful service and volunteer experience, and earn some money.

Admissions Advantage or Life Advantage?

Just about everything you do to prepare for college has bigger life implications, too.

1. When you work hard in your classes in high school, you become better educated.

2. When you find and commit yourself to activities you enjoy, you discover your talents, learn to work with other people, and enjoy life outside of the classroom.

3. When you learn how to do something for yourself without relying on your parents, you become more independent and better prepared to live on your own.

4. When you find a subject that interests you and dive in to learn more, you see just how rewarding learning can be when you let your interests guide you.

5. When you struggle in a class and approach your teacher for help, you learn how to advocate for yourself and how to seek out assistance when you need it.

6. When you try your best and still come up short, you learn how to handle that failure or disappointment, learn from it, and then move on.

7. When you take all of these lessons with you to college, you get more out of the overall experience.

Chapter 5

Financial Aid & Scholarships

What is the FAFSA? 114

What is my Expected Family Contribution?.................................117

What's the CSS/Financial Aid Profile? 118

What financial information do I need to apply for financial aid
  using the FAFSA and/or the CSS Profile?..................................119

How does the financial aid application process differ from the
  admission process? 121

What is in my financial aid package?...122

What is the difference between need-based and merit-based
  financial aid?...125

How do I look for scholarships? 126

How do I save/pay for college?...127

If my first-choice school's online college calculator shows that I can't
  afford it, should I bother applying? 129

What is a need-blind school?...134

Will I be penalized if I apply for financial aid? Will colleges look
  favorably on me if I don't apply for financial aid?....................136

Can I appeal my financial aid decision?......................................138

Is it a smart move to attend a two year / associates degree–granting
  school first to save money?...139

CHAPTER 5
Financial Aid & Scholarships

The financial aid process is complicated enough, and the rising costs of college does not make it any easier. The average sticker price (tuition, fees, room and board) for one year at public four-year colleges in 2021–22 was $22,690 (for in-state students)—a 1.8% increase over the previous year. At private four-year colleges, the average was $51,690—a 2.1% increase. More than 70 colleges now have a sticker price of $70,000 (or more). Those numbers sound scary, and I often hear families make assumptions like, "We can't afford private schools," or "We'll never qualify for aid." Be careful—aid assumptions like those tend to work against you when it comes to paying for college. Rather than just looking at the sticker price, carefully read through the financial aid pages on the colleges' websites that interest you. Once you see what types of financial aid are available, you may find that more colleges are accessible than you thought possible.

Here's the bottom line: Assuming your family can't pay for some (or any) colleges just takes options off the table. Feeling discouraged could lead you to feel less motivated to work hard on your application, or disregard certain colleges that are right for you, which are often the schools most likely to give you aid! Ultimately, you won't know what your financial obligation will be until after you are accepted, apply for financial aid, and receive your financial aid award letter. So, as you factor the cost for college into your search, make no assumptions. Plan well, choose the right colleges, and apply for any aid that's available to you. In this chapter, I will answer the questions that I get asked most frequently regarding financial aid. Please understand that the subject of how to pay for college is a big one! This topic needs more than just a comprehensive chapter to fully address all of your questions and concerns. I strongly recommend reading *Paying for College*, watching my YouTube videos, and reading the articles on PrincetonReview.com.

What is the FAFSA?

You'll hear about the FAFSA a whole lot during the college admissions process. This is the Free Application for Federal Student Aid. It's a long form that collects student and parent financial information and is used to determine the student's eligibility for financial aid. Even if you don't think you're eligible, you should still submit the form, just in case—you have nothing to lose.

When applying for college, you do not need to complete the FAFSA for each school where you plan to apply. You will be able to list up to ten schools on the application to receive the relevant information. You will need to complete the FAFSA each year you require aid. The form is updated each year and made available on October 1, for use in the following academic year. The FAFSA is available online, on paper, or as a downloadable PDF at studentaid.gov. College financial aid deadlines vary. I strongly recommend submitting your FAFSA at the same time as your application for admission, and submitting it as soon as possible after October 1 each year thereafter.

> Crafting an appeal is a delicate art and should only be undertaken if you have a strong case for revisiting your aid decision.

The financial information you enter on the FAFSA will cover the amount of money you and your parents or guardians made during the calendar year two years before you enter college—this is called the "base income year" on the FAFSA. You may also see it called the Prior Prior Year (PPY), which refers to the year before the prior tax year. For a student entering college directly after high school, financial aid eligibility will be based on their family's financial situation during 10th grade second semester and 11th grade first semester.

Take note: Your family may have experienced a decrease in income between the base income year and your FAFSA submission, which makes that base income year totally irrelevant to your current situation. The good news is that colleges are allowed (although not required) to use *another* 12-month period of income that is more "representative" of a parent's current situation. My friend Kal Chany, author of *Paying for College,* advises that if a parent or guardian is making less money for any reason, you should ask for a reevaluation by explaining your changed circumstances in a letter, which you will submit *after* you get a financial aid package. (We'll talk more about appealing financial aid decisions later on in this chapter). Be prepared to provide documentation of that lower income. Some schools will ask you to fill out a special appeal form that they've created. Provide as much supporting detail as you can and be sure to clearly and succinctly explain your situation. That will improve your chances of a successful outcome.

Average Cost of College

Average cost of a year's tuition, room and board, and fees in 2021–2022

Private College: $51,690

Public (In-State) College: $22,690

*College Board, *Trends in College Pricing, 2021*

When you complete the FAFSA, you will receive a Student Aid Report that summarizes the financial information you provided and shows your Expected Family Contribution (EFC), or the amount your family will be responsible for paying toward your college costs. (I go into EFC in more detail on the next page.) Your Student Aid Report also will show your eligibility for different types of federal student aid. You may also be eligible for state financial aid and / or for aid granted directly by the school. Federal aid is based on adjusted gross income and assets (like property and investments). Some states base financial aid eligibility on taxable income and do not take other assets into account. All fifty states have need-based aid programs and about half offer merit-based aid, which is awarded based on your academic record and test scores instead of on your financial situation. In most cases, to be eligible for state aid, you must attend a private or public college or university within your state of residence. In some states, aid is awarded on a first-come, first-served basis, so it benefits you to apply early.

I know it sounds complicated, but financial aid is just another part of the college admission process that we can crack through research and planning.

What is my Expected Family Contribution?

When you complete the FAFSA, the federal financial aid methodology determines how much your family can afford to put toward your college education based on their income and assets. This is the Expected Family Contribution amount on your Student Aid Report. Your EFC is the same no matter where you go to school or how much that school costs. The total cost of any college includes tuition and fees, room and board, personal expenses, books and supplies, and travel—as determined by each college or university. The difference between the total cost of attendance and your EFC is called your "need." Colleges and universities offer a wide range of aid packages to cover that need, which is why I always discourage families from crossing schools off their list early in the application process based on sticker price.

> I always discourage families from crossing schools off their list early in the application process based on sticker price.

You can find financial aid and EFC "calculators" online, in which you can enter a sampling of the information you will provide on your FAFSA and find estimated college costs based on your financial situation. These can be helpful in getting oriented in college planning, but take the resulting figures with a healthy pinch of salt. Calculator methodology varies from site to site and the results are not guaranteed, even when the calculator is hosted on the college's own website.

What's the CSS/Financial Aid Profile?

CSS stands for College Scholarship Service. This is another form that collects your financial information to determine your financial need for college, and it goes into more detail than the FAFSA does. Your state and/or some private colleges may require the CSS Profile in addition to the FAFSA, while public institutions typically rely exclusively on the FAFSA to make financial aid decisions. The CSS Profile is created by the College Board (the same entity that writes the SAT and AP Exams), and unlike the FAFSA, it entails application fees. Colleges that require the CSS Profile are not trying to punish you with extra forms and fees. These schools have additional financial aid resources beyond federal funds, and their financial aid officers want to have a detailed picture of your finances so that they can try to help you cover your college costs. Institutions that rely on the FAFSA use the federal methodology to determine your eligibility for aid, while those that use the CSS most likely have their own institutional methodology. You should contact a specific school's financial aid office with any questions about their financial aid form requirements, methodology, and decision-making process.

When you complete the CSS Profile (which you can do on cssprofile. collegeboard.org), instead of a Student Aid Report, you will receive a Data Confirmation Report summarizing your information and confirming which schools received it.

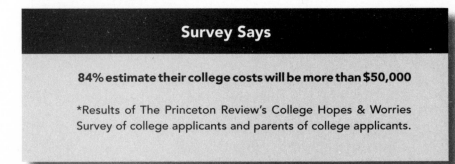

Survey Says

84% estimate their college costs will be more than $50,000

*Results of The Princeton Review's College Hopes & Worries Survey of college applicants and parents of college applicants.

What financial information do I need to apply for financial aid using the FAFSA and/or the CSS Profile?

For the FAFSA, you will need:

1. Completed federal tax return for the base income year (two calendar years before you or your student will enter college)

2. W-2 forms for the base income year

3. Records of any untaxed income for the base income year, if applicable. Examples include social security, welfare, tax-exempt interest

4. Bank statements for the base income year

5. Brokerage statements for the base income year, if applicable

6. Mortgage statements for any properties other than your primary residence for the base income year, if applicable

7. Student's social security number (and driver's license number if the student has one)

8. Any financial statements or corporate tax returns for businesses owned by parents or entrepreneurial applicants for the base income year

9. Other investment statements and records for the base income year

10. Records of child support paid or received during the base income year

For the CSS Profile, in addition to the 10 items above, you will also need:

11. Records of medical and dental expenses paid during the base income year

12. Records of any post-secondary tuition paid or that will be paid during the academic year before the year for which you are applying for aid

13. Records of any educational loan payments made or to be made during the two calendar years prior to the year for which you are applying for aid

14. Mortgage statements for your primary residence for the base income year, if applicable

15. Financial aid awarded to any member of your household, if applicable, for the academic year prior to the year for which you are applying for aid

Schools offering great financial aid (alphabetical order):

- Brown University
- California Institute of Technology
- Carleton College
- Denison University
- Grinnell College
- Hamilton College
- Haverford College
- Pomona College
- Princeton University
- Rice University
- Vanderbilt University
- Wellesley College
- Williams College
- Yale University

PrincetonReview.com/college-rankings/financial-aid-honor-roll

How does the financial aid application process differ from the admission process?

	Admissions	Financial Aid
Application	• The Common Application OR • The Coalition Application OR • School's own application	• FAFSA • CSS/Profile if required • State form if required • School's own form if required
Decisions based on	• Test scores, if required • GPA • Rigor of high school courses • Recommendations • Essays • Extracurriculars • Supplemental application material	• Your and your guardians' financial picture
Deadlines *confirm exact deadlines for both application and financial aid with the schools on your list*	• Regular decision: Typically Jan. 1 • Early decision: Typically Nov. 15	The latest date you can file a FAFSA is June 30th of the academic year for which you are applying, but most colleges request that all aid forms are completed with your admission application. I recommend submitting your financial aid forms ASAP after October 1.

What is in my financial aid package?

Your financial aid award letter will include details on the combination of aid that the school can offer to meet your demonstrated financial need. There are three types of aid:

Grants and Scholarships

Grants and scholarships consist of money that you won't have to pay back! Grants may be funded by the federal government, the state, or the college. Grants are tax-free. Most scholarships are awarded by the college or university, and may include eligibility criteria, like meeting a GPA threshold or participating in an extracurricular leadership development program. Some schools are more transparent than others about the amount of grant money available to students, which is usually based on the school's endowment and aid policy. Some schools guarantee grants or scholarships for accepted students who meet GPA and test score thresholds. Some find creative ways to give aid to all of their students. Cooper Union in New York, NY, awards every student who attends a scholarship to cover half of their tuition, and all students are automatically considered for additional merit-based aid. Berea College in Berea, KY, awards every admitted student a Tuition Promise Scholarship, which is combined with financial aid to cover the full cost of tuition. (Keep in mind that tuition does not include room and board, personal expenses, or travel.) At Guilford College in Greensboro, NC, every new student is offered at least $15,000 a year in financial aid. These are just three examples of schools with strong public track records of awarding generous financial aid.

> Even with favorable borrowing and repayment terms, be wary of accruing debt in college, and take out private unsubsidized loans as little as possible.

Student Loans

Education loans are typically taken out by students rather than their parents. Federal and state loans are often subsidized, with guaranteed below-market interest rates, by the government. You won't have to pay back the loans until you graduate, and many loan programs offer income-based repayment options. Even with favorable borrowing and repayment terms, be wary of accruing debt in college, and try to avoid using private unsubsidized loans if possible.

Federal Work-Study

This is a program through which the government provides money to the school to fund part-time jobs on campus for students. The money you earn through a work-study job goes to tuition and/or living expenses. It's also an opportunity to gain

> The money you earn through a work-study job goes to tuition and/or living expenses.

valuable work experience—many schools guarantee jobs to students who are eligible for work-study, and these experiences can help you find more lucrative summer employment and/or build your resume. The financial aid office will have a list of open positions and guidance on applying. Jobs will likely run the gamut from food prep in the cafeteria to handling confidential information in the development office.

8 Quick Tips for Getting Financial Aid

1. **Learn how financial aid works.** The more and the sooner you know about how need-based aid eligibility is determined, the better you can take steps to maximize such eligibility.

2. **Apply for financial aid no matter what your circumstances.** Some merit-based aid can only be awarded if the applicant has submitted financial aid application forms.

3. **Don't wait until the student is accepted to apply for financial aid.** Do it when applying for admission.

4. **Complete all the required aid applications.** All students seeking aid must submit the FAFSA (Free Application for Federal Student Aid); other forms may also be required. Check with each college to see what's required and when.

5. **Get the best scores you can on the SAT or ACT.** They are not only used in admission decisions but they can also impact financial aid. If your scores and other stats exceed the school's admission criteria, you are likely to get a better aid package than a student with marginal scores and stats.

6. **Apply strategically to colleges.** Your chances of getting aid will be better at schools that have generous financial aid budgets. (Check the Financial Aid Ratings for various schools on PrincetonReview.com.)

7. **Don't rule out any school as too expensive.** A generous aid award from a pricey private school can make it less costly than a public school with a lower sticker price.

8. **Take advantage of education tax benefits.** A dollar saved on taxes is worth the same as a dollar in scholarship aid. Look into Coverdell, 529 Plans, education tax credits, and loan deductions.

*From *Paying for College* by Kalman Chany. See the Appendix for all 26 of Kal's financial tips.

What is the difference between need-based and merit-based financial aid?

"Need-based" financial aid is determined by your household finances and intended to cover the difference between your Expected Family Contribution and the total cost of attending college.

"Merit-based" financial aid is determined by the college or university that has accepted you based on your academic, athletic, or artistic talent, and may be awarded regardless of your demonstrated need (that means it can lower your Expected Family Contribution). Merit-based aid is typically referred to as a grant or a scholarship, depending on the awarding institution. When you are researching deadlines for each of the schools where you plan to apply, make a note of any scholarships for which you might be a competitive candidate and their deadlines, as in some instances specific scholarships may have earlier application deadlines than regular admission or financial aid applications.

> When you are researching application deadlines for your prospective colleges, make a note of any scholarships for which you might be a competitive candidate and their deadlines.

How do I look for scholarships?

The best place to look for scholarships is within the institutions to which you are applying. Most schools work to fund and award scholarships and grants based on a variety of criteria, and many automatically consider you for merit-based grants or scholarships when you apply for admission and submit your FAFSA. If you want to pursue a scholarship, though, don't assume it will be a snap; ask the admissions officers at the school of your choice how many scholarships are awarded each year, how many students apply for scholarships (or the one scholarship you have your eye on), and if the scholarship is renewable. Some scholarships are only for first-year students. Some are renewable each year, but only if you maintain a certain GPA, pursue a specific major, or continue to compete on the varsity basketball team (for example).

Scholarships from sources outside the college or university account for less than 5% of the financial aid awarded in the United States.

A few good places to look for scholarships outside of colleges and universities are your city/town/municipal government, your parents' or guardians' employers, and any professional or philanthropic organizations to which they might belong. Scholarships from sources outside the college or university account for less than 5% of the financial aid awarded in the United States. That is still a lot of money (a total of $235 billion in student aid was available to undergraduate and graduate students in 2020–2021), but overall, your odds of using an outside scholarship to pay for college are low.

If you are considering using a scholarship search service that charges a fee, please, please, please vet it very carefully. While some of these services are legit and have been a boon for their users, some are simply charging for information you can find for free with a little legwork.

How do I save/pay for college?

To be completely frank, this topic deserves a book of its own, and happily, my friend Kal Chany has written that book, *Paying for College*. It's packed with investment tips for saving money for college and line-by-line strategies for completing the FAFSA to help you maximize your eligibility for financial aid. In lieu of trying to pass myself off as a financial advisor here, I'm presenting some helpful tips and an overview of calculating college costs in the future.

If you're reading this book in high school, hopefully your family has already started saving when it comes to your college tuition. Don't worry if that's not your situation; there are a lot of options for paying for college, especially if you focus on earning high test scores and grades. While financial aid is based primarily on demonstrated need, applicants who are especially desirable to a college because of their strong academic performance or athletic or artistic talent may receive preferential packaging—basically, a more lucrative financial aid package, whether it's a higher total amount or is comprised of more grants or scholarships than loans.

No matter when you plan to attend college, if you're not already saving, start now. Every little bit helps, and if you can put your money into a high-yield investment or savings account, it will earn compound interest—that means more money for college. If your parents are saving for you, their accounts and investments should be in *their* names—putting that money in your name could impact your eligibility for financial aid.

Calculate Your Costs

According to the College Board, as of 2021–2022, the average sticker price (tuition, fees, room and board) for one year at a public four-year college (in-state) was $27,330. One year at a private four-year college will cost more than twice that, at $55,800. The current rate at which college costs are increasing is less than 4% per year—believe it or not, this has fallen off from the average annual increases of 3.9% and 5.0% over the two prior decades. While we can't predict the future with perfect accuracy, we can use these figures to calculate useful estimates.

It's worth noting that we're looking at average figures, and many top colleges have already crossed the $70,000-a-year barrier. The more you can save for college, the more options you will have available to you. You do not need to be a millionaire to obtain a college degree, however—during the 2019–2020 academic year, 86.4% of college students received some form of financial aid.

If my first-choice school's online college calculator shows that I can't afford it, should I bother applying?

Applying doesn't mean accepting a school's offer, so the short answer here is yes. Here's why:

The requirement that all colleges and universities participating in federal financial aid programs must have a net price calculator on their website is a huge step forward when it comes to financial transparency. This is a great help for students and families when it comes to estimating the net price for attending college. It is a good tool in your decision-making toolbox, but it shouldn't be the *only* one.

The trouble with college net price calculators is their lack of uniformity. The federal government requires that universities have a net price calculator available, but it doesn't require that all colleges have the same one. Because there is no standardization across different colleges' net price calculators, your comparisons may be apples-to-oranges based on each school's unique criteria and the financial and academic information you're asked to submit. Consequently, some net price calculators are better than others. Usually, the more detailed the questions, the more accurate the estimate.

The current federal net price calculator template is a good starting point, and it takes some personal factors into account, but not everything. For example, the federal template does not ask students for their high school GPA, which could help predict merit-based grants. The same goes for talent-based aid, such as athletics or fine arts scholarships. Also, keep in mind that net price calculators may not reflect current market conditions, student enrollments, or endowment levels. They typically use the previous academic year's information, but some schools use older academic years, and the amount of money a school has for financial aid can differ significantly from year to year.

You'll want to approach the calculators with a critical eye to see how much information they request from you—and how personalized the results are. Remember that these are estimates. The actual price you pay may be higher or lower than the college's net price calculator estimate. A 2021 peer-reviewed study[10] by the University of Pittsburgh found that the prices determined by net price calculators vary by an average of $5,700 per student for students from families with the same or similar economic situations. So, use the college's net price calculator, but keep in mind that it is an *estimate*.

It's worth it to apply to your first-choice school to find out what you are actually offered in their financial package. And sometimes the financial aid offer can be improved. Last-minute scholarship money may become available if other accepted students end up going elsewhere. It's wise to check back nearer the acceptance deadline to find out whether more money has become available. In addition, you can try using leverage to get more financial aid. Schools can get competitive with each other for top students. If your second-choice college offers you more money, it never hurts to ask your first-choice college if they will match the offer. However, make sure you understand the details of both financial aid award packages. For instance, you may find one school is awarding you more money for the first year, but the other is offering you more money over the course of your entire college career.

Here's a real-world example to consider:

Brown University tuition for the 2021–2022 school year: $60,944

Average freshman total need-based gift aid: $54,823

You're probably sick of calculators by this point, so we've done the math for you: that's an average of $6,121 for the year. Now, that doesn't include the cost of room and board—don't forget to include those in your final calculations!—but that's a far more palatable price tag. Some schools are incredibly generous with financial aid, so do your research before writing off any. The Princeton Review website has some great financial aid information including a list of the Top 20 Best Schools for Financial Aid (Private Schools) and the 14 colleges on our Financial Aid Honor Roll (PrincetonReview.com/college-rankings/financial-aid-honor-roll). Another good resource to consider is *The Best Value Colleges*, the most recent version of which can be found on our website (PrincetonReview.com/college-rankings/best-value-colleges).

---

[10] direct.mit.edu/edfp/article/16/4/716/101981/How-Big-is-the-Ballpark-Assessing-Variation-in

Financial Aid Terms You Need to Know

1. **Financial Aid:** A general term referring to programs that serve to assist students with their educational costs. Funds can come from the federal and state governments, as well as the individual schools. While the names may vary, financial aid comes in three basic forms: (1) gift aid (grants and scholarships) that does not have to be paid back (2) student loans, and (3) work-study jobs.

2. **Cost of Attendance:** A figure, estimated by the school, that includes the cost of tuition, fees, room, board, books and supplies, as well as an allowance for transportation and personal expenses. This figure is compared to the Expected Family Contribution to determine a student's aid eligibility.

3. **Expected Family Contribution (EFC):** The amount of money the family is expected to contribute for the year toward the student's cost of attendance. This figure is compared to the Cost of Attendance to determine a student's aid eligibility.

4. **Parent's Contribution:** The amount of money the parent(s) are expected to contribute for the year toward the student's Cost of Attendance.

5. **Student's Contribution:** The amount of money the student is expected to contribute for the year toward his or her cost of attendance.

6. **Need:** The amount of aid a student is eligible to receive. This figure is calculated by subtracting the Expected Family Contribution from the Cost of Attendance.

7. **Need Analysis Forms:** Aid applications used to calculate the expected family contribution. The most common need analysis forms are: the Free Application for Federal Student Aid (FAFSA) and the CSS/Financial Aid Profile form. Consult the individual school's financial aid filing requirements to determine which form(s) are required for that particular school.

8. **Free Application for Federal Student Aid (FAFSA):** The need analysis document written by the U.S. Department of Education. This form is required for virtually all students seeking financial aid including the unsubsidized Stafford loan (see 17).

9. **Student Aid Report (SAR):** The multi-page report that is issued to students who have filed a completed FAFSA.

10. **CSS/Financial Aid Profile:** A need analysis application created and processed by the College Board. Also known as the CSS Profile or the Profile form.

11. **Institutional Forms:** Supplemental forms required by the individual schools to determine aid eligibility.

12. **Gift Aid:** Financial aid, usually a grant or scholarship, that does not have to be paid back and that does not involve employment.

13. **Grants:** Gift aid that is generally based on need. The programs can be funded by the federal and state governments as well as the individual schools.

14. **Pell Grant:** A federally funded need-based grant program for first-time undergraduate students (i.e., the student has not as yet earned a bachelor's or first professional degree). Funds from this program are generally awarded to lower- and lower-middle-income families.

15. **Scholarships:** Gift aid that is usually based on merit (academic and/or talent) or a combination of need and merit.

16. **Self-Help:** The portion of the aid package relating to student loans and/or work-study.

17. **Direct Loan Program:** Formerly known as the Stafford Student Loan program, this federally funded program provides low-interest loans to undergraduate and graduate students. In most cases, repayment does not begin until six months after the student graduates or leaves school and there are no interest charges while the student is in school. For new loans disbursed after June 30, 2006, the interest rate is fixed. (Prior loans had variable rates.) There are two types of Direct loans: subsidized and unsubsidized. The subsidized Direct loan is need-based and the government pays the interest while the student is in school. The unsubsidized Direct loan is non-need-based and can be taken out by virtually all students. In many cases, students can elect to let the interest accumulate until after they graduate.

18. **Parents Loans for Undergraduate Students (PLUS):** A federally sponsored educational loan program in which parents can borrow up to the total cost of attendance minus any financial aid received for each child in an undergraduate program. Eligibility is not based on need.

19. **Federal Work Study (FWS):** A federally funded aid program that provides jobs for students. Eligibility is based on need.

What is a need-blind school?

"Need-blind" means a college or university makes admission decisions without taking into account an applicant's financial situation. A school may also be "need-sensitive" or "need-aware," which means that finances are considered in admissions in order to ensure that the school will be able to offer financial aid to those students who need it. While taking finances out of the admissions process may sound like a fairer process given how hard you're working on your grades and test scores, it can be disappointing for students who are accepted but find their demonstrated financial need is not met by their financial aid package.

> A need-blind admission policy is most meaningful when it is combined with a commitment from the school to meet every accepted student's demonstrated need.

For applicants, a need-blind admission policy is most meaningful when it is combined with a commitment from the school to meet every accepted student's demonstrated need. In most cases, these policies only apply to U.S. applicants, due to the college's resources and the fact that international students are not eligible for federally funded aid. There are currently only seven colleges in the U.S. that extend need-blind, full-need admissions for both U.S. and international students: Amherst College, Curtis Institute of Music, Harvard College, MIT, Princeton University, Yale University, and the Minerva Schools at KGI (part of the Claremont University Consortium)—all highly selective schools with very competitive applicant pools. The remainder of the Ivy League is need-blind for U.S. students, need-sensitive for international students, and will meet the full demonstrated need for all accepted students. An additional thirty-seven selective schools follow the same policies (some examples: Duke University, Rice University, and The University of Chicago). Some public universities will only consider in-state students under need-blind, full-need policies, but not out-of-state students.

Survey Says

What's the biggest concern of students and parents about applying to college?

41% say level of debt to pay for the degree

28% say will get into first-choice college, but won't be able to afford to attend

24% say won't get into first-choice college

7% say will attend a college I (my child) may not be happy about

*Results of The Princeton Review's College Hopes & Worries Survey of college applicants and parents of college applicants.

Will I be penalized if I apply for financial aid?
Will colleges look favorably on me if I don't apply for financial aid?

These two questions are asking the same thing: At colleges and universities that are need-blind, do students who can pay full freight for four years have an edge when it comes to gaining admission? Sometimes. If you know you will need financial aid to complete your degree and your dream school is need-blind, you might consider adding a need-aware college to your list.

Need-Blind vs Need-Aware Admission	
Need-Blind Admission	An applicant's ability to pay for their education will not be a factor in the college's decision to admit, wait-list, or deny the applicant. Need-blind admission doesn't require that an applicant with demonstrated financial need be awarded financial aid, nor does it require that 100% of the applicant's demonstrated need be met.
Need-Aware Admission	Colleges do consider an applicant's ability to pay for their education when making admission decisions. This control can allow colleges to meet full need for all accepted students.

Ultimately, these policies should not play a major role in choosing the colleges that fit you best. Most colleges and universities do not give your finances significant weight in admission decisions. You are better served focusing on the college's academic offerings and extracurricular resources when choosing where to apply, and working on your grades and test scores to increase your chances of acceptance.

Need-aware admission policies also do not provide strategic leverage on your application. The only scenario where the ability to pay for college can meaningfully impact your college decision is if your application lands in the "maybe" pile at a need-aware institution. In that case, being able to pay full sticker price may help move you into the "accepted" category. If you have a lackluster transcript and average test scores, your bank account is not going to get you into college. If you will need financial aid and anticipate that you are eligible for it, you should apply for it and answer any relevant questions on your college application honestly (the Common Application asks if you will be applying for aid or not). If you indicate on your application that you will not need aid and get accepted, you won't be able to apply for financial aid later—the school's financial aid office will have already apportioned the aid available for the year. It doesn't matter if you get into a great school if you can't pay for it (and taking on loads of debt to pay for college isn't a great idea for your financial future).

> The only scenario where the ability to pay for college can meaningfully impact your college decision is if your application lands in the "maybe" pile at a need-aware institution. In that case, being able to pay full sticker price may help move you into the "accepted" category.

Can I appeal my financial aid decision?

Yes, but doing so requires a delicate approach and sound reasoning. If the financial aid package you have received works for your financial situation, you are unlikely to be granted additional funding. Parents, you may pride yourselves on your business negotiation or bargaining skills, but you'll find that financial aid officers can't be tricked or pressured into giving you a better financial aid package. If, however, the package offered by your dream school is prohibitively low, or if you are trying to decide between two schools with similar reputations that have offered you different aid packages, it may be worth approaching the financial aid office for a discussion. You won't be risking your initial offer in doing so.

> Send in your appeal as soon as possible after the financial aid package arrives.

Below, find our tips on appealing your financial aid decision, culled from *Paying for College.*

1. **Timing is everything.** Send in your appeal as soon as possible after the financial aid package arrives. The sooner the better!

2. **Reach out.** Call the financial aid office or ask for an in-person meeting if it's an option. Ask to speak to or meet with the head of the office, if possible.

3. **Get prepped.** Have copies of your FAFSA and other financial aid forms on hand, as well as any other aid offers you are considering.

4. **Be honest.** Any claims you make about your finances or another school's offer must be backed up by documentation.

5. **Be polite.** Aggression or confrontation will not earn you any love from financial aid officers.

Is it a smart move to attend a two year/associates degree–granting school first to save money?

I've heard more and more questions like this as college costs have increased dramatically in recent years and families are experiencing sticker shock. If your goal is to obtain a bachelor's degree but you're finding that a four-year school seems cost-prohibitive no matter how you crunch the numbers, you might consider starting at a community college or public in-state university and applying to transfer to your dream school after one or two years. The total cost of your degree will be significantly lower than four years of private college. You will be more likely to transfer your credits from a four-year degree program to the school that will ultimately award your degree than from an associate's or two-year program—and, in the event that plans change, you're still on track to a bachelor's degree. (I dive into transfer applications in Chapter 8.)

> If you plan to begin your degree at one school and graduate from another, it is essential that your pre-transfer grades are excellent.

One caveat: Transferring colleges can be trickier than applying right out of high school. If you plan to begin your degree at one school and graduate from another, it is essential that your pre-transfer grades are excellent. Make sure you leverage every possible resource for academic support, whether that's the university writing center, a professor's office hours, or peer tutoring.

9 Creative Ways to Pay Less for College

1. **Attend a community college for two years and transfer to a pricier school to complete the degree.** Plan ahead: Be sure the college you plan to transfer to will accept the community college credits.

2. **Look into "cooperative education" programs.** Over 900 colleges allow students to combine college education with a job. It can take longer to complete a degree this way, but graduates generally owe less in student loans and have a better chance of getting hired.

3. **Take as many AP courses as possible and get high scores on AP exams.** Many colleges award course credits for high AP scores. Some students have cut a year off their college tuition this way.

4. **Earn college credit via "dual enrollment" programs available at some high schools.** These allow students to take college level courses during their senior year.

5. **Earn college credits by taking CLEP (College-Level Examination Program) exams.** Depending on the college, a qualifying score on any of the thirty-three CLEP exams can earn students three to twelve college credits.

6. **Stick to your college and your major.** Changing colleges can result in lost credits. Aid may be limited to or unavailable for transfer students at some schools. Changing majors can mean paying for extra courses to meet requirements.

7. **Finish college in three years, if possible.** Take the maximum number of credits every semester, attend summer sessions, and earn credits via online courses. Some colleges offer three-year programs for high-achieving students.

8. **Let Uncle Sam pay for your degree.** ROTC (Reserve Officer Training Corps) programs available from U.S. Armed Forces branches (except the Coast Guard) offer merit-based scholarships up to full tuition via participating colleges in exchange for military service after you graduate.

9. **Better yet:** Attend a tuition-free college.

*From *Paying for College* by Kalman Chany

As you can see, financial aid and figuring out how to pay for college requires more than just a chapter; you need at least an entire book to cover the topic! Hopefully, this overview has answered some of your most pressing questions and has pointed you in the right direction to get the information you need. There are many books and resources available to you, including *Paying for College: Everything You Need to Maximize Financial Aid and Afford College,* online *Best Value Colleges* lists and articles at PrincetonReview.com, and my multiple videos about financial aid and paying for college on The Princeton Review YouTube channel.

Chapter 6

Application

What is the Common Application?..145

Are there other applications like the Common Application?
Is one better than another? 147

What do admission officers look for in an application essay? 150

How do I write a game-changing college essay?..152

When should I start the application process? 154

Should I declare a major on my application or apply undecided?...................156

How important is optional or supplemental application material?.................157

Is a college interview required? What should I expect? 158

Who should I ask to write my letters of recommendation?...............................161

CHAPTER 6
Application

To become a competitive college applicant, you have three jobs to do while you're in high school:

1. Be awesome academically and take on a challenging work load.
2. Do well on standardized tests.
3. Research colleges to equip yourself with as much information as possible.

Of course, there's still one more activity you'll need to complete if you want to go to college—the actual process of applying to college.

What is the Common Application?

The Common Application is an online app that you can use to submit your information to multiple schools. Nearly 900 colleges and universities accept the Common App. While different schools often use different essay prompts or ask you to answer additional questions in shorter form, all schools need your contact details, the name of your high school, a list of your extracurricular activities, some information about your family, and so on. Having a tool that allows you to create a profile of this information that you can send to most, if not all, of the schools on your list is a major time saver. When I applied to college, I had to enter the same information about ourselves over and over on paper forms by hand! The Common App also makes it easy to keep track of which documents you've completed and submitted to each school.

The Common App is updated for each academic year on August 1. You can create an account at commonapp.org. Be sure to confirm each school's specific admission requirements, like the number of recommendation letters you'll need, which, if any, test scores, and school-specific forms or essays, as well.

Since 2020, to address the universal impact of the coronavirus crisis, the Common App has provided students with the space to explain how the pandemic has affected them personally and academically. The world is constantly changing, so be sure to check commonapp.org for their most up-to-date changing, so be sure to check commonapp.org for their most up-to-date guidelines. Here is the question in full:

Community disruptions such as COVID-19 and natural disasters can have deep and long-lasting impacts. If you need it, this space is yours to describe those impacts. Colleges care about the effects on your health and well-being, safety, family circumstances, future plans, and education, including access to reliable technology and quiet study spaces.

- *Do you wish to share anything on this topic? Y/N*
- *Please use this space to describe how these events have impacted you.*

The space is yours to explain a dip in your science grade as you got used to your new remote classroom or how the new family responsibility of watching your younger siblings after school barred you from joining the French Club as you'd planned.

4 Tips for Managing College Application Stress (from Real Students Who Have Been There)

1. **Mark everything on a calendar.** "Create a schedule for application and scholarship deadlines and prioritize by the due dates."

2. **Be open-minded.** "College is about finding your happiness, not your parents' happiness or what would look good on your bumper."

3. **Keep the end goal in mind.** "Don't get frustrated with applications. Just think of how good you'll feel in the fall walking the halls of your chosen college."

4. **Ask questions.** "Guidance counselors, your parents, and your friends are there for you to help with your stress levels and the college decision process. While you may feel alone with your emotions over college, the people you are surrounded with have probably felt the same way you do now."

*Results of The Princeton Review's College Hopes & Worries Survey

Are there other applications like the Common Application? Is one better than another?

There are a few similar application options for smaller cohorts of schools. ApplyTexas is an application system for public universities and many other institutions in Texas; California uses one system for all the University of California schools and another system for all Cal State University schools. There is also an alternative to the Common App called the Coalition Application that is accepted by 140 colleges and universities. The information on the Coalition App will be substantively similar to what is collected on the Common App, but the digital interface is different. The Coalition Application makes it simple to apply for application fee waivers and provides online tools you can use to share your application materials for feedback with your teachers and counselors.

Some colleges use one application type exclusively. Others may accept either the Common Application or the Coalition Application and might have a proprietary application in the mix, too. If a school accepts more than one type of application, you should choose the option that works best for you—admission officers do not prefer one over the other.

> If a school accepts more than one type of application, you should choose the option that works best for you—admission officers do not prefer one over the other.

The Coalition Application app addresses COVID a little differently than the Common App, but the goal is the same: to communicate to colleges how the pandemic affected your family circumstances from dealing with illness to losing an after-school job. This time you'll have an optional "check-all-that-apply" style question, plus an optional text field if you choose to say more. Here's the question text in full:

Natural disasters and emergency situations like the COVID-19 pandemic have impacted the lives of many students and their families. While entirely optional, you may share information here regarding how any of these events have affected you or your family circumstances.

Check all of the following that apply to you:

❒ *I had inconsistent or unreliable access to home internet and/or a computer, laptop or tablet.*

❒ *At least one parent/guardian lost their job or was unable to work.*

❒ *I lost my job or was no longer able to work.*

❒ *At least one parent, guardian or caretaker was considered an essential worker (e.g. healthcare worker, grocery store employee, public transportation driver, first responder, sanitation worker) and was required to work.*

❒ *I was considered an essential worker and required to work.*

❒ *My community had a curfew affecting the hours I could travel, use electricity, or access the internet.*

❒ *My home responsibilities (i.e. childcare, elder care, etc.) substantially increased or changed.*

❒ *My health was affected.*

❒ *A member of my household's health was affected.*

❒ *None of these apply to me.*

❒ *I would like to provide additional information. (Text box appears providing for 300 words max)*

Types of College Applications

	What is it?	School examples:
The Common Application	A single online college application form used by over 900 colleges and universities.	• Stanford University • The College of William & Mary
Coalition Application	A single online college application and digital portfolio used by the 140 member schools of the Coalition for Access, Affordability, and Success.	• University of Pennsylvania • Yale University
Universal College Application	A single online college application used by 4 colleges and universities.	• Harvard College • Cornell University
College-Specific Applications	Many university systems or schools have their own exclusive application.	• University of California (UC Application) • University of Texas (ApplyTexas)

Note: Many colleges accept more than one type of application. For example, Harvard College accepts the Common Application, the Universal College Application, or the Coalition Application.

What do admission officers look for in an application essay?

First and foremost, application readers want to know that you can write. That doesn't mean you need to use a lot of big words or flowery metaphors. Your sentences should be clear, your ideas organized and logical, and your grammar, punctuation, and spelling should be flawless. Patience, revision, and proofreading will help you refine these aspects of your essay. Start writing early and give yourself time to work through a few drafts.

What to write about is another matter, and one of the more overwhelming and anxiety-inducing aspects of the admission process. Most schools that require essays will provide a writing prompt, or a few prompts to choose from, but many of the prompts or questions used are open-ended enough that you can write about almost anything. Choose something that is important to you and will give you opportunities to tell admission officers about yourself. You should be able to explain why the topic or experience matters to you and how it has influenced you.

Take note: Many students are likely to write about their experience during the coronavirus pandemic for the next few years, which might make it harder to distinguish yourself to the admission committee if you take that essay route. There are many other topics that demonstrate the depth and breadth of who you are! (Check out our book *The Complete Guide to College Application Essays* for tons more advice on this front). Plus, both the Common Application and the Coalition Application have added COVID-specific questions to allow students who want to write about the pandemic a place to do so apart from their main essay.

It's also important that your voice comes through in your essay. You don't need to be overly ambitious with your writing style or form, and a tone that feels affected or inauthentic may work against you. Think about how you would tell the story of your essay in a face-to-face interview. When you write with language that doesn't come naturally to you, it shows, and your essay may feel strained and miss the mark.

YOU should write your essay, not your older sibling or a parent or private admission counselor. That said, you will want to solicit feedback and proof-reads from at least two other sets of eyes. Getting feedback on your work will help you craft a stronger essay, and extra eyes will help you catch typos.

Don't go overboard with input, though—too many conflicting opinions and suggestions can make you doubt your instincts and result in a flat essay that feels written-by-committee.

If you are applying to several schools, be very careful when re-using essays on different applications. You may need to make small tweaks to your main essay for each school. Make sure the essays you're submitting are responses to the school's prompts, and ALWAYS double-check any school names in your essays or short answers—many, many admission officers have told me about receiving essays in which the applicant has left in a mention of another college. That's a fast track to the rejection pile.

5 Tips for College Essays

1. **Tell the story that grades and test scores can't capture.** A thoughtful and sincere essay about something that's important to you—an experience, a person, or a book—shows colleges the unique qualities you will add to the incoming class.

2. **Always be yourself in your application, not the candidate you think admission committees want to see.** Sometimes it's better to write about an experience that was hard for you because you learned something, rather than writing about something that was easy for you because you think it sounds impressive.

3. **Remember to reflect.** You're not the only applicant to win the class presidency, go on a service trip, or suffer an athletic injury. Take the opportunity to really examine how an experience taught you something you didn't previously know about yourself, got you out of your comfort zone, or forced you to grow.

4. **Start early, and write several drafts.** Coming up with an original, thoughtful essay topic will inevitably take a fair amount of brainstorming. Make sure you start writing early in the application process.

5. **Ask a parent, teacher, or friend you trust to be your editor.** The more time you spend with a piece of your own writing, the less likely you are to spot errors (and your college essays must be 100% typo free!).

How do I write a game-changing college essay?

College essays are a fantastic opportunity to distinguish yourself from other applicants. There may be other applicants with similar grades and test scores, but there is only one YOU! You get to show colleges—in your own voice—the personality, character, and feelings that make you the unique person you are. Schools want to see what sets you apart from your peers, and so they genuinely want to know the distinctive qualities and experiences that make you tick. This is especially true for schools with holistic acceptance processes—those that place less emphasis on standardized test scores—where they want to know how you might fit into their community and contribute to their school.

Our *Complete Guide to College Application Essays* book offers a variety of activities meant to help you brainstorm, develop, and edit your ideas, and I heartily recommend working with someone to help polish and perfect your essay. It's also a good idea—especially if you're going to be submitting through the Common App—to look at the given sample prompts on their website so that you can make sure the story you want to share fits.

If you're still not sure where to begin, start by doing a freewrite on the subject. For instance, you might list some of the turning points in your life. They don't need to be major events, but each should be an occurrence that genuinely affected you. Consider the people you've met, places you've traveled, books you've read, and media you've interacted with, so long as it's made a difference to you.

Remember, you don't have to write about the extraordinary to BE extraordinary. One student I know wrote about her love of showering and got into Yale. What's important is that you're authentic and clear about your values and goals, how you deal with challenges, and what matters most to you. Make sure to include a clear summary, specific details that awaken the reader's senses, and a reflection that serves to connect your story to the prompt. I know this may seem like a lot, so take it one step at a time and keep this key piece of advice in mind: if you are bored while writing your essay, your readers will be as well.

More College Essay Tips

Consider your reader. In this case, your reader is an admissions officer who is reading through hundreds of college essays. You don't want to bore that person, but don't be controversial or sensational for its own sake. However, it's fine to take a risk if you're sharing a unique viewpoint or a strong conviction that you hold dear.

Avoid extremes of tone. Humor and creativity can certainly set your essay apart, but make sure they don't compromise your message. Your reader's sensibilities may not be the same as yours, and you don't want to push them away.

Avoid regurgitating your resume. This is not the place to talk about your academic career or write your entire life's history. Use this opportunity to share what ISN'T in the rest of your application.

Stay within the required—or suggested—length. This shows that you can follow directions. Most essays are not very long; they average about 650 words.

Get it perfect. Even if you're submitting your essay within an online application, you don't have to write it there. Use the program that you're most comfortable with and take full advantage of a word counter and spellchecker before copying-and-pasting the final version. Just remember to check the formatting once you're done!

When should I start the application process?

Ideally, you should be thinking about college throughout high school, choosing courses and extracurriculars that will set you up to be a competitive applicant, researching and visiting (online or in person, if possible) in your junior year, and preparing for the SAT and/or ACT before the start of your senior year.

> The more time you give yourself to craft a strong application, the less stressed out you will feel and the more options you will have if something comes up.

As for completing the application itself, my advice has always been to start early, and this has been echoed by many parents and students on our annual "College Hopes & Worries" survey over the years. The more time you give yourself to craft a strong application, the less stressed out you will feel and the more options you will have if something comes up. If you are completing the Common Application, you can start working on it as early as August 1st (Note: In recent years, the Common App has announced its new essay prompts for the upcoming academic year as early as February, so keep a lookout and you may be able to start drafting your essays even earlier). If you are applying for financial aid, you will be able to start the FAFSA as early as October 1. College application deadlines vary, but typically Early Decision deadlines fall in early November and Regular deadlines fall in early January. If any of the colleges on your list have rolling admissions, applying as early as possible can help give your application a boost. Rolling admission means that applications are accepted over a few months, and admissions decisions are made as applications are received, instead of all at once following a cut-off date. So, there are a lot more spots open at those schools early in the application time frame than there will be closer to their final deadline.

Another good reason to begin preparing your application materials early is that you will need to rely on other folks or systems to obtain some materials, and this can take a bit of time. Your high school is processing requests for academic transcripts for all your peers applying to college, so confirming that your transcripts have been sent may take a few days or weeks. If you have concerns about your standardized test scores, you may want additional time to prep for and retake the SAT and/or ACT. Like transcripts, your official score reports will take a few weeks to reach the colleges where you're applying. Once you've completed the FAFSA, and the CSS Profile, if necessary, the official analysis of your financial information can take up to four weeks before it is provided to your schools. And don't forget about letters of recommendation. You should give your letter-writers at least a month to draft and submit your recommendations, especially if you know they are writing recommendations for many other applicants.

College Essay Advice (from a Real Student Who Has Been There)

"Once the Common Application or specific college applications open, look over the essay questions and requirements. Begin gathering ideas and outlines for them over the summer after junior year. Have rough drafts as early as possible to begin editing and accommodating the word counts."

—College Hopes & Worries Survey

Parent to Parent

College to Career

"We pick schools in an upside down fashion. We pick a school based on reputation, then find a major we think we might like, and then four years later try to shoehorn a career around it.

The better way—determine the career, understand which major will best lead to that career, then find the school that does the best job for that major/career."

—College Hopes & Worries Survey

Should I declare a major on my application or apply undecided?

Unless you are applying to a specific school within a university or unique program dedicated to an academic track, you do not need to declare a major on your college application. If you do inform the admissions office of what you'd like to study, no one will hold you to that later if you change your mind. In most liberal arts academic programs, students must declare a major by the end of sophomore year. If you don't know what major to choose, you'll have time to evaluate the different academic offerings (and work towards any general education requirements) at your school during your first two years, and you'll spend your junior and senior year focusing on the requirements for your major.

It's common for parents and applicants to believe that declaring a major on a college application matters in the admission decision. Some people think that declaring a major shows focus and passion, and helps to communicate what you will bring to the campus community. Some people worry that admissions officers have quotas for different majors, and that committing to something popular like English may work against them if many other students have chosen the same major. In most cases, admission officers do not expect the majority of high school seniors to have their careers mapped out, nor will they penalize you if you do know what you want to study. If you must declare a major on your application and it will be considered inside the admissions office, the school will make that clear.

If you do know what you want to study, go ahead and include that in your application. The more information admission officers have about you, the clearer it will be that you're a great fit for their school.

College Major Advice
(from a Real Student Who Has Been There)

"Still go to college even if you do not know what you want to study. Don't let the unknown scare you because you might find out your passion in college."

—College Hopes & Worries Survey

How important is optional or supplemental application material?

It's right there in the name: optional or supplemental.

If you don't submit any additional information or achievements outside the required application materials, the lack thereof won't work against you. If you have not found a place in your application to share an interest, pursuit, or accomplishment, this is your chance to do so—it never hurts to provide admission officers with additional information on your strengths and skills.

> If you don't submit any additional information or achievements outside the required application materials, the lack thereof won't work against you.

Optional or supplemental application material is a great way to share something visual with admission officers, like an art portfolio, a video of a theatrical performance or debate team competition. Visual media has the additional value of helping you stand out in both the applicant pool and an admission officer's mind.

You don't need to leverage optional/supplemental material for anything that would be redundant with other parts of your application. If you're required to submit an academic writing sample with your application, you don't need to submit a second sample here. If you've won academic awards or athletic competitions and these are listed on your application or appear in your essay, there's little benefit in restating these achievements here. Admission officers are incredibly busy during application season, and most aren't able to give optional/supplemental material more time and attention than the average application receives. If your application is a complete and accurate picture of you, you've done a great job and don't need to add anything additional. If you do want to submit additional material, make sure that it's adding something to your application, that it can be understood quickly by busy admission officers, and that you follow the school's directions for submitting material to a T.

Is a college interview required? What should I expect?

Interview requirements differ from school to school. Many colleges and universities offer applicants the opportunity to interview on campus or via video conferencing with a member of the admissions team or with an alum who has been trained to conduct interviews. Often interviews are optional or encouraged rather than required. If you are able to interview, whether it's required or not, I recommend that you do! This is another opportunity to make an impression on the admissions committee and share what you can uniquely bring to campus. Many colleges are expanding their virtual interview options, so take these opportunities when they are offered!

A college interview is also helpful to make sure the school where you're applying is a good fit for you. Your interviewer is representing the campus community, so if you connect with them, that's a good sign. It's also an awesome opportunity to ask in-depth questions about the school that you haven't been able to answer through your research. Not only will you get some info that you want, but you'll show the interviewer that you're curious, informed, and invested in attending the school. Try to avoid asking generic questions or questions that you could easily find the answer to online.

Be specific when you talk about your interest in the school. Why does it feel like a good fit for you? What about it stood out during your visit or research? Alumni who conduct admission interviews are typically people who valued their college experience and remain involved with the community—they love their alma maters, and they want to know that you will, too.

With any interview, you should prepare for commonly asked questions, and try to practice with a parent, teacher, or counselor to make sure you know your talking points and feel comfortable adapting if you get a question you're not expecting. You want to present yourself as confident and comfortable, but also as professional and poised. If you've interviewed before for a job or internship, you have valuable experience. If you haven't yet, your college admission interview will be a valuable learning experience you can draw on in future job interviews.

For video interviews, you should always prepare your home "interview space" in advance. So, set up your computer in a clean, well-lit (and quiet!) corner of your house, test that your computer's microphone and camera are in working order, and dress for the part of eager college hopeful.

Interview Tips (from Real Students Who Have Been There)

Don't just take my word for it. Here are some smart tips from last year's crop of college applicants.

1. **Interviewers know sincere enthusiasm when they see it.** "Before you apply to any college, learn about all the reasons that make you want to go there. This really helps as not only will this be used in the interviews but also in your application; your application must talk about you, and how you see yourself in the college."

2. **Politeness pays off.** "Always send 'thank you' notes."

3. **Be true to you.** "Colleges want to know how you are as a person, so in interviews and such, just be yourself! Show them your awesome identity!"

4. **Show them you're serious.** "If you are really interested in a college, let them know! Request an informal alumni interview before interviewing with an admissions counselor."

5. **Knowing you're prepared will help you relax.** "Take many deep breaths. Practice and go into interviews with confidence!"

*Results of The Princeton Review's College Hopes & Worries Survey

College Interview FAQs

If you're ready to discuss these seven topics, you'll be ready for your college interview.

1. What's an example of a challenge that you overcame, and what did you learn from it?

2. What's your favorite high school class and why?

3. Tell me something about you that I wouldn't know from your application.

4. What do you plan to study in college? (Hint: if you're undeclared, that's totally okay—this question gives you an opportunity to talk about different majors or careers you are considering and how you might go about choosing a major if you're accepted.)

5. Why do you want to attend this college or university?

6. What do you enjoy doing when you're not in class?

7. Do you have any questions for ME?

Who should I ask to write my letters of recommendation?

While your grades, test scores, and transcript will always be the most crucial parts of your application, letters of recommendation are very important. These letters represent professional adults, usually teachers and school counselors, who are endorsing your academic performance and your future plans. You will probably need at least two letters of recommendation from teachers you've had for academic subjects (as opposed to electives), though some schools ask for three recommendations or offer you the option of submitting additional letters of support from coaches, employers, or counselors. These recommendations are submitted directly to the school—you won't get to see them before the admission officers do.

You will want to choose your recommenders wisely; you don't have to ask the teachers who gave you the best grades. In fact, a teacher who has seen you face challenges and has supported your growth would be in a terrific position to write you a recommendation. You should choose teachers with whom you have a connection and who are familiar with your academic track record. If you're unsure who to ask for recommendation letters, you should talk through your options with a parent or your high school counselor. If you're reading this book in 9th or 10th grade, think about how you might build relationships with teachers you like. Look for opportunities to ask for extra help or work with the teacher outside of class, and think about your class participation. Do you have a lot to say in class? How does the teacher respond? You'll want to build similar relationships with your college professors and eventually with work superiors, so this is a skillset that you will use throughout your life.

Plan ahead and approach these tasks professionally. Chances are you are not the only student asking for a recommendation letter during application season, so be sure to give your recommenders enough time to draft and submit your letters before the deadline. They will either need to mail signed hard copies or use online tools to securely submit their letters (both the Common App and Coalition App have options for submitting recommendation letters online). When you ask your teachers to write you recommendations, you should have any materials (forms, addressed stamped envelopes), deadlines, URLs, and submission instructions they will need to submit letters on time. I recommend that you also offer a list of extracurricular activities, a draft of your college essay, and any other info that you think might be relevant. This will help give your teacher fodder for their letter and put their recommendation into the full context of your application. It's especially helpful if you're approaching a teacher you had before senior year—you can update them on your latest accomplishments. Finally, don't forget to be polite when you ask for letters, and send a thank you note for the letter once you've submitted your application. It's poor form to wait until you're accepted by the college to say thank you, but you should absolutely let your recommenders know when and where you get in—they're invested in your admission process, too.

How to Ask for Letters of Recommendation

Emailing your teacher at 2 A.M. two weeks before the application deadline to ask for a letter of recommendation? Not good. Here are some better rules of thumb:

1. **Check with your high school counselor first.** Some high schools have established systems they want their students to follow for requesting letters of recommendation.

2. **Ask early.** Preferably as early as possible in your senior year or even in your junior year (once you have the necessary materials).

3. **Give details.** Give your teacher some indication of why you are asking them, in particular. I recommend giving your teacher a list of your extracurricular activities, a draft of your application essay, and any other information you think is important so they have ideas for what to write in the letter.

4. **Be exceedingly polite.** Remember, you're basically assigning your teachers homework. Above all else, be kind, considerate, and appreciative when interacting with your teacher.

5. **Send your teachers each college's specific instructions and deadlines.** You may need to fill out a form from the college, provide credentials and information for a college's online application system, or get an addressed and stamped envelope.

8 Questions to Ask Your High School Counselor

Your high school counselor is your #1 resource for college prep and applications. Here are some questions to kick off the process.

1. What classes should I take in high school?

2. Am I on track for graduation requirements?

3. Are any colleges visiting our high school this year?

4. What are some appropriate colleges for me to look at?

5. What extracurricular activities can I get involved with?

6. What do I need to fill out the FAFSA?

7. Can you help me find local scholarships?

8. Do you have any special instructions for students requesting transcripts, counselor reports, or letters of recommendation?

Chapter 7

Inside the Admissions Office

What are my chances of getting into my dream school?...................................167

How are my application materials reviewed?.....................................169

Who is on the admission committee?...171

What is the single most important thing admission officers look
    for in an application?...172

Will applying Early Decision or Early Action give me a leg up?.....................174

What does it mean to be deferred?
    What can I do to improve my chances of acceptance? 177

What if I don't get accepted to my first-choice school? 179

What are my chances of getting off the waitlist?.............................180

Do admission officers look at prospective students' social
    media accounts?...181

How much weight do schools put on intangibles like "grit"? 183

Inside the Admissions Office

In this chapter, we take a look behind the curtain at what goes on inside a college admission office. You've hit send on your application, your transcripts and scores have all been mailed—now what? Let's investigate the review process, including who is actually reading your application, how they make a decision, and what next steps you can take in the event of an admissions roadblock like being deferred or waitlisted.

What are my chances of getting into my dream school?

To honestly assess your chances of getting into a college, you need to find out how you stack up to the students who go there. Carefully research each college's admission standards and compare your GPA, SAT and/or ACT scores, class rank, and high school courses to see if schools you are considering are a good academic fit. Colleges publish averages for their most recently accepted first-year class on their websites, and you can also find these stats in the college profiles on PrincetonReview.com.

> To honestly assess your chances of getting into a college, you need to find out how you stack up to the students who go there.

You'll also want to check out the school's acceptance rate, which will put those other numbers (GPA, test scores, etc.) into perspective:

- If the acceptance rate of a school is at least 50%, and your GPA and test scores are about the same as the middle range for the first-year class, you can consider that a "target school." It's not a guarantee you'll get in, but the odds appear to be in your favor.

- If the acceptance rate of a school is between 35% and 45%, your grades and test scores would need to be near the high end of the range to consider that a target school.

- Any college that accepts fewer than 20% of the applicants is a highly selective school and usually a reach for just about everybody.

This isn't an exact science, as many of these schools will also be looking at activities, letters of recommendation, essays, and your interview, all of which can influence a decision.

But what is a "dream school" anyway? If you mean that, based on all of your research, your dream school is your best-fit school academically, campus culturally, as well as financially and from a career services perspective, then your chances of earning admission should be excellent for the simple fact that you've done your homework.

That's really the ideal—finding a place where you say "YES, that's the school for me!" and "YES, that's the place that suits me best!" Sometimes, it's easier said than done, as you might imagine. Sometimes it's easy to get wowed by a school's brand name and the perception that a school in and of itself is going to guarantee you an awesome and successful future.

The truth is that no school can ever make that guarantee, but you have the ability to earn those lofty levels of success at any school you choose. It sounds simple, and it is. Provided you do the digging and the honest research through that best-fit lens and resist defining your dream school solely on brand or admission selectivity, then you're going to do oh so well!

On Dealing with Rejection (from a Real Student Who Has Been There)

"There is a place for everyone. Relax and think of it as a journey—not a race to be won, but a home to be found."

—College Hopes & Worries Survey

How are my application materials reviewed?

What does go on behind closed doors once your application reaches the admissions office? The answer is not so simple, because colleges and universities use their own formulas. At some schools, the evaluation is an exercise in number-crunching. If you've taken the required classes, cleared the minimum GPA, and earned the minimum tests scores, you're in. Other schools undergo a more personal evaluation. They use your application to get a sense of who you are beyond the numbers and how you might contribute on campus.

Here's an example of how it works at many colleges and universities:

A student's application is handed off to an admissions officer (a "reader") for a preliminary reading. Most readers start by reviewing the rigor of your classes, the grades you've earned, and your test scores. They'll look through your essays, read your letters of recommendation, peruse your extracurriculars, and consult your interviewer's report, if applicable. During this time, readers may take notes on each part of the application and write a summary of your strengths, weaknesses, and anything else that was compelling or interesting about you.

At many schools, if you're clearly admissible (meaning your high school GPA and standardized test scores, etc., sit well within or above the mean for accepted students at that school), then the decision to admit you might well rely on the positive recommendation of that first reader. The recommendation can be reviewed by others on the admission team, but basically, you've cleared the first major hurdle!

Same drill on the other end of the spectrum, if your high school GPA, standardized test scores, etc., are well below the mean, then the initial recommendation of the first admissions officer to deny your application will likely stick. Don't forget, though: colleges will absolutely consider the extenuating circumstances behind any drop in grades or test scores (for example, a rocky transition to remote learning at your high school).

If you make it past the first reader, it's possible that a second reader may weigh in and compare their impressions with those of the first reader. Some applications may be accepted right then if both readers agree on the application, some may be sent to another senior admissions officer to review, and some may be sent to the larger committee for discussion.

If your application makes it to this point, at least one of the admissions officers wants to admit you! But all of the other admissions officers have applicants they want to admit, too, and at selective colleges, they can't admit everybody. Your admissions officer will plead your case by summarizing the most compelling parts of your application—anything from your riveting application essay to a single line in a recommendation letter that makes them think you will thrive at their college. They'll fight for you.

Of course, different schools will use different variations of the system described above, but there's one constant: real humans will evaluate you. When they do, they'll look at lots of things beyond just grades and test scores.

Who is on the admission committee?

As the name implies, your admission decision doesn't rest on the whim of just one person, but it is likely in the hands of many. What a relief, right? It's good to remind ourselves that the admission review process is a VERY HUMAN process at lots and lots of schools.

Admission committees are comprised of the admission officers responsible for reading and evaluating applications from your high school (and other high schools in your state, region of the country, etc.). It's common for colleges to group applications by geographic area so that each reader is evaluating students from a particular region, allowing readers to get familiar with the high schools in their assigned areas.

Of course, different colleges have different systems. At some, undergraduates and faculty members play a role. At others, all decisions are made by a small handful of professionals. At still others, decisions are made democratically by large committees. Depending on the size of the college, a school's director of admission, dean of admission, vice president of enrollment (and other top brass) may all weigh in on your application. Suffice it to say that more than one person will be evaluating your application. Since the admission process can be so subjective—both for applicants and admission officers—that's a good thing!

What is the single most important thing admission officers look for in an application?

The #1 most important piece of information that a student will submit on their college application is universal to all schools (public, private, large, small, etc.). The answer is your high school GPA/high school transcript. OK, that's clearly two different things. But, they're definitely related!

> You can never underestimate the power and raw heft of your high school transcript and GPA.

Going forth after reading this answer, you can never underestimate the power and raw heft of your high school transcript and GPA. Your high school transcript is the weightiest of documents in your application because it's a complete record of your academic achievements in four years of high school. The document contains your cumulative GPA for all four years, but also the classes you took and the grades you received in each of those classes. Most importantly, your transcript answers these questions: Have you consistently challenged yourself academically throughout high school? Have you challenged yourself with regular courses? Honors classes? APs? IBs? No, this doesn't mean you have to take every single Advanced Placement class or that you can never take a fun and easy elective (not that there's anything easy about ballroom dancing, trust me). However, admission counselors are looking for evidence that you're willing to undertake challenging coursework on a consistent basis—evidence that you'll do well in college. Never underestimate the importance of your high school transcript in the college admission process.

Of course, just signing up for impressive classes won't cut the mustard—you'll have to do well in these courses, too. While it's true that it looks better to take difficult classes and not always get sky high grades than to take easy classes and always excel, a high overall GPA is crucial. What to do if you have poor grades? It's time to light a fire under them and heat them up. Don't think that just because your grades are low, everything's lost. Most college admission offices look favorably on students who start off poorly but then work to raise their grades.

I suspect you're wondering what the second most important piece of information that you'll submit with your application might be. This one does waiver a bit from school to school, but it's still solidly the second most reported important piece of info. The answer is standardized test scores—the SAT and ACT being the most important.

How to Evaluate Your Admission Chances

1. **Research the college's most recent first-year class.** Search for your college on PrincetonReview.com/college-search (or find the "Class Profile" on the college's own website).

2. **Know what stats to look for.** Find these pieces of information about the college's current first-year class:

   - The SAT/ACT range for the middle 50%

   - The average high school GPA

   - How many freshmen were in the top 10%, 25%, 50%, etc., of their high school class

   - The overall percentage of applicants accepted

3. **Interpret the data.** The acceptance rate of a college gives you an idea of where your GPA and test scores need to be to have a good chance of admission.

Will applying Early Decision or Early Action give me a leg up?

I really want to give you a direct and universal answer to this question, but it's not so straightforward. The truth is that the answer varies from school to school. That said, the broad brush strokes I go into below will give you some perspective.

But first, let's dig into the terminology.

Many colleges allow applicants to submit their materials for an early deadline (sometime in the fall) that falls before the regular deadline (usually sometime in January or February).

> **Early Decision** is binding. This means if you are accepted through early decision, you are committed to attending that school and will withdraw any applications you may have submitted for the regular deadlines at other schools. However, if you have a good reason for backing out of an early decision offer from a college, the school *may* let you leave without penalty. A common reason for being released from the offer is financial—if a student doesn't receive the financial aid package or grants they need and therefore can't afford to attend the school. Be aware that you may not apply to more than one college under early decision. If you are not accepted, you will either be rejected or deferred. Rejected applicants may not apply again that year. Deferred applicants will be reconsidered during the regular admission period and are free to apply to other schools (More about deferred admission coming up). Early decision deadlines are often in November, and students are typically notified of the decision in December.

> **Early Action** is non–binding. This means you are not bound to attend if you are accepted. You may also apply early action to multiple colleges. Early action deadlines usually fall at the same time as early decision.

Early Admission Strategies

Most early decision schools (that is, schools that offer an early decision admission option) admit between 10% to 20% of their incoming freshman classes as early decision. Hence, the majority of students are admitted through the regular decision channel.

However, there is an increasing number of early decision schools (many offering Early Decision 1 and Early Decision 2 deadline alternatives) that admit 30% to 45% of their freshman classes early decision! At those kinds of schools, it makes it harder for students to be admitted through the regular decision channel. Early decision could offer a leg-up at such schools.

Early action has all the value of early decision but few of the obligations. That's attractive from a student perspective (general sigh of relief) but offers little from the admission strategy perspective. The obvious advantage of early action over early decision is the opportunity it gives you to apply to, and ultimately compare, financial aid packages from several schools. If you are accepted early decision, you risk missing the admission deadlines of other schools while you wait for your award package to arrive. If that award is lackluster, your options are fewer.

If you're sure that you've found your best-fit school, you know it's one you want to attend, you're a strong candidate for admission, and you know that you can afford the tuition, go ahead and apply early decision.

That is a whole lot of research and comparison to have done by fall of your senior year, though, and if you're uncertain about any of those factors, you're not alone! Keep your options open by applying early action or by the regular deadline.

College Admission Options

Application Type	*Deadline	Is the decision binding?	If you're accepted, when do you decide?
Regular Admissions	On or around January 1	No	May 1
Rolling Admissions	Within the school's "application window," usually a 6-month period between August and March	No	May 1
Early Decision	November 1 or 15	Yes	N/A. Early decision is binding. If you're accepted, you're going!
Early Action	November 1 or 15	No	May 1

*ALWAYS double-check deadlines with each of your prospective schools. The deadlines listed here are approximates.

What does it mean to be deferred? What can I do to improve my chances of acceptance?

First off, being deferred doesn't mean that you've been denied. Generally, students receive deferrals if they've applied to a school through early decision or early action channels. If a school doesn't admit a student outright through those early channels (most don't), your application moves to (is "deferred to") the regular decision channel.

In my book, a deferral to that regular admission channel means opportunity! You're done with the hard work, and your application is already in the regular admission pool at your first-choice college. So, take heart. A deferral is an indication that the admission committee thinks your qualifications are solid. They are just getting a sense of the full applicant pool for the year. That same admission committee will review your application in full (again) in roughly two month's time.

Deferred? Here's what to do.

- If you haven't had an admission interview (should a school offer them), then do it!

- Remember that admission counselors reviewing your application in the regular decision channel will be reviewing your newest high school marking period grades and any new standardized test scores. Your academic awesomeness will have a chance to shine yet again!

- Here's another way to be proactive. In late January or early February, compose a letter or email to the school and ask that it be included with your application materials. The letter should provide an update on your activities since the early application deadline. Include your first semester grades and any academic highlights, new developments in your extracurricular activities, and your plans for the rest of senior year. Request an interview if you haven't had one yet. Then, reiterate your undying love for this school above all others, all the reasons why you are a great fit, and your commitment to enroll if admitted.

- Full steam ahead (with regular decision applications, that is). Remain optimistic, but create your contingency plan. You already have the foundation of a great college application. You probably already have a list of schools that you considered on your way to choosing where to submit that early application. Revisit that list. Does it include schools that suit your interests and goals? Schools you can afford to attend? Schools where you're likely to gain admittance? Prepare applications for regular decision deadlines with the same attention to detail you invested in your early application, and submit them on time. Hold out hope that you get into your top choice, but aim for acceptance at a few other schools so you have some to choose from in the spring.

What if I don't get accepted to my first-choice school?

I'm not going to lie; rejection hurts.

It may help to know that you are in good company; most students will be rejected by at least one of the colleges they applied to. And if your first choice was a top-tier, highly selective school (20% or less acceptance rate), that means 80–95% of the students who applied weren't admitted. In fact, it's harder than ever before to get accepted into selective universities, and schools that were perhaps more accessible to, say, your parents may now seem out of reach. (Take UCLA, for instance: in 1995, they took 40% of applicants, but in 2021, they admitted only 14%.)

Many factors go into the college admission process that are beyond your control. It's possible that your dream school couldn't accept any more students from your state, or they needed more athletes, tuba players, or had some other need that they had to fill.

Not getting into your top-choice school does not reflect your worth or capability. Knowing this may not lessen the sting of not being admitted and of having to change all your plans, and it's okay to take some time to feel disappointment (or even devastation). Find a healthy way to grieve this loss—it's okay to cry, lean on family and friends, watch a lot of movies—and then turn your energy toward the options that are in your control.

One of the reasons we recommend applying to multiple schools is so that you have several fantastic schools to choose from. Once you've gotten a handle on your disappointment, take a look at the institutions that did accept you, and start remembering what got you excited about them in the first place. If there are features that aren't offered at these schools, consider drafting proposals to the one you choose or look toward organizing them yourself where possible. (This is great real-world experience that'll look terrific on job applications.)

Your dream school is not the only place where you can get an excellent education, make lifelong friends, and have amazing experiences. Disappointing as it may be to wake up from a dream, making the most of reality can be even more rewarding.

What are my chances of getting off the waitlist?

I'm a glass half full kinda guy, but I would be dishonest if I told you the chances were good. Nationally, relatively few applicants placed on a waitlist receive admission.

But first, let's make sure we're all on the same page about what a waitlist actually is. All selective colleges admit more students than they have room for. They do this because they know that many of the students they admit won't actually enroll. Guessing how many students will enroll is a very inexact science. To protect themselves, most colleges have a waitlist. An applicant who is "waitlisted" is one who may be admitted if enough students decide to go somewhere else.

If you're waitlisted at a school you want to attend, there are some things you can do that can help your case substantially. Write a letter or email reaffirming your desire to attend the school. Ask your college counselor to call the admission office. Send a letter describing any honors you've won and other achievements since you sent in your application. When colleges admit students from the waitlist, they almost always give preference to students who make it crystal clear that they really want to attend.

At the most selective schools, admissions from waitlists are sometimes few and far between. Harvard College, for example admitted zero students from the wait list for the 2020–2021 academic year. Princeton University admitted 26 waitlisted students and California Institute of Technology admitted ten. We're all human and should recognize that it's a tough thing to reconcile in our heads. Here's the silver lining, though. If you curate a list of schools to which you'll apply (six to eight is the average number of applications submitted by individual students), then you need to be sure that you'd be thrilled (really, I mean it, THRILLED) to attend any one of them if admitted.

How much weight do schools put on intangibles like "grit"?

"Grit" is a buzzword that has been popular among educators and admissions officers in recent years. My own opinion is that "grit," an amorphous quality comprised of character and commitment, is great, but it's not actually a new element for college applications—admissions officers have been looking for it in candidates for a long time. It is commendable that schools are making attempts to quantify, measure, and develop "grit" in students, but I think it comes through on college applications whether we have a specific definition and measurement or not.

It's my belief that a college application adds up to more than the sum of its parts—ultimately, your grades, test scores, recommendations, extracurricular activities, essays, interviews, and supplemental material tell a story about you. All of the advice in this book is intended to help you see your application, and yourself, as a whole, not a collection of statistics and checkboxes. When you are able to put your achievements and your passions together effectively, the story your college application tells is about your character, your interest in challenging yourself, and your ability to persevere.

> All of the advice in this book is intended to help you see your application, and yourself, as a whole, not a collection of statistics and checkboxes.

By taking the most challenging classes available to you, utilizing your resources to earn the highest grades and test scores possible, building positive relationships with your recommenders, and articulating your interests, experiences, and growth through essays—you're showing college admission officers that you've got "grit."

Chapter 8

8

Etc.

Is the admission process different for international students?........................187

How difficult is transferring between colleges?..190

Should I take a gap year before starting college? 194

What if I need additional accommodations (and will requesting them
hurt my chances of admission)? 197

How highly should I weigh a school's stance on social and ethical issues? 200

What impact will cheaters have on my admissions chances? 202

How can a parent participate most effectively in their child's
college application process?..204

How do I balance schoolwork, extracurriculars, test prep,
college applications, family, social life, and SANITY?!....................................208

CHAPTER 8
Etc.

These questions don't fit nicely into a tidy chapter, but I am asked them all the time. From deciding if a gap year is right for you to maintaining your sanity during college admission season, here's everything (else) you need to know.

Is the admission process different for international students?

The admission process is a little different for international students, yes.

For one, most U.S. universities require international students to submit scores from an English language proficiency exam, like the TOEFL (Test of English as a Foreign Language) or IELTS (International English Language Testing System). Admission officers want to know that you can succeed in courses delivered in English, even if English is not your first language and if your education was not in English. This also means that many schools place a greater importance on the college essay, another demonstration of English skills.

Otherwise, the factors for admission decisions are largely the same as those for domestic students: grades, test scores, and the strength of your high school curriculum. (For a refresher on crafting competitive applications, refer back to Chapter 7.)

> The admit rate for international applicants is a bit lower than the overall admit rate, and the field can be competitive.

The admit rate for international applicants is a bit lower than the overall admit rate, and the field can be competitive. According to NACAC's 2019 *State of College Admission* report[11], the international student admit rate is 52%, while the

---

[11] https://www.nacacnet.org/news--publications/publications/state-of-college-admission/

admit rate for first-time freshman students is 66%. Of course, the acceptance rate for international applicants will vary school by school and can be much lower, especially at public universities. Do your research before you apply!

School	Total undergraduate enrollment	% international students in student body	# foreign countries represented
University of Pennsylvania	9,872	13%	126
Harvard College	5,187	11%	104
Massachusetts Institute of Technology	4,550	10%	103
University of Michigan—Ann Arbor	31,189	7%	91
Virginia Tech	29,893	6%	116
Georgia Institute of Technology	15,740	9%	116

Data reported to The Princeton Review by the school from fall 2020 to spring 2021

According to the 2021 Open Doors Report, the total number of international students at U.S. universities dropped by 15% from 1,075,496 in 2019–2020 to 914,095 in 2020–2021.

Financial Aid for International Students

You should also keep in mind that for students who are not U.S. citizens or eligible non-citizens, financial aid possibilities are limited. No federal aid, for example, is given to nonresident aliens, although schools are free to give out their own grants and scholarships. It's possible that financial aid may not be available for international students through the universities you are considering (this depends on the college).

Check with all the schools on your list to find out what their filing requirements are for international students. Many colleges will ask that you complete special aid forms designed specifically for international students. Some of these colleges will also require a Certificate of Finance, which is issued by the family's bank and details the sources and amounts of funds available to the international applicant.

How difficult is transferring between colleges?

Plenty of students transfer between colleges every year. In fact, about one-third of all students will swap institutions at least once before earning their degree.

> Transferring colleges can be a great move if you're sure that the new school offers opportunities your current school lacks.

Transferring colleges can be a great move if you're sure that the new school offers opportunities your current school lacks. That said, transferring involves an application process, and competition for open spots can be fierce, especially at prestigious and highly selective schools.

First, let's look at why some students decide to transfer.

1. **They're unhappy.** One excellent reason to transfer is because you are unhappy. If you find that the school you are attending is not the best-fit college for you, you don't have to settle for four years of misery. Now that you have more clarity about what you want out of your college experience, you are even better equipped to find one that will meet your academic and social expectations.

2. **They want to pursue an academic or career interest that's not supported at their current school.** Another reason to transfer is if your current school does not have a strong program in your major or area of interest. If you've decided to be a doctor and your college has a weak pre-med program, don't be afraid to look elsewhere.

3. **They want another shot at their first-choice college.** Some students who are rejected from their first-choice school attend another school with the intention of later transferring. Others begin their education at a two-year community college but ultimately want a four-year degree.

4. **They want to save tuition dollars.** A student might decide to enroll at a less expensive school so they can save money, and then transfer to a more expensive school after one or two years. This strategy can save families thousands of dollars and make a financial reach school more affordable.

If your goal is simply to enroll in a college with bigger name recognition, you might want to reconsider. The difference in reputation between your old school and your new one may not justify the time and effort of transferring.

Transfer Applications

If you do end up deciding to transfer colleges, you'll fill out another college application (this time it might be a designated Transfer Student Application or the Common App for transfer application, depending on the school). That's right—you'll collect letters of recommendation, submit test scores, and write another round of essays.

There are, however, some key differences from applying to colleges the first time around.

- For one thing, your high school transcript and test scores will take a back seat to your college transcript. Standardized test scores are used (in theory) to predict college grades. Once you have college grades, the scores are less important. So, earn strong grades in college if you hope to transfer (some schools will still want to see your SAT or ACT scores as well).

- Colleges have different policies for transfer students but typically expect you to have acquired a minimum number of credits. You'll have a harder time transferring if you've completed more than two years of study, even if you abandon some of the credit you've accrued.

- Colleges usually expect transfer applicants to have clear, compelling academic reasons for wanting to switch schools. The best reason is a strong desire to pursue a course of study or experience that isn't offered at your present school. You'll have to make your case in detail and be convincing. A transfer applicant, unlike a first-year applicant, can't get away with being "undecided" about academic or career goals.

- Transferring can impact your intended graduation date or study abroad plans. Be aware of the policies at your prospective transfer school. Not all classes/credits are transferable, and some schools won't accept credit from a class if you earned below a C.

Financial Considerations

Typically, transfer students are eligible for less scholarship funds than first-year students, though some schools set aside money specifically for transfer students. If you go this route, be sure to ask your prospective schools about their financial aid policies. You'll want to make sure your transfer college is a great financial fit!

Transfer Acceptance Rates

Okay, back to the original question. How difficult is it to transfer? According to NACAC's 2019 *State of College Admission* report[12], the transfer acceptance rate is slightly lower than the freshman acceptance rate. Of course, your odds of acceptance as a transfer student can differ on a school-by-school basis, as you can see in the chart on the next page. It's often significantly more difficult to be accepted to a selective school as a transfer student than it is right out of high school. In fall 2020, MIT, for example, accepted around 7% of freshman applicants but only 3% of transfer applicants.

---

[12] https://www.nacacnet.org/news--publications/publications/state-of-college-admission/

School	# of applicants	% applicants accepted	# of transfer applicants	% transfer applicants accepted
Stanford University	47,498	4%	2,216	4%
Harvard College	40,248	5%	1,376	1%
Massachusetts Institute of Technology	21,706	7%	673	3%
Duke University	35,767	9%	1,274	5%
University of Michigan— Ann Arbor	65,021	26%	4,513	46%

Data reported to The Princeton Review by the school from fall 2020 to spring 2021

To boost your chances, keep those grades up, and use some old-fashioned interpersonal methods: contact college admission officers directly, and keep in touch with them.

Should I take a gap year before starting college?

There are several things to consider if you're deciding whether or not to take a gap year—that is, a year off between high school and college. A year off can seem exciting ("A break from studying, woohoo!"), but to some, it may feel scary ("I don't want to derail my trajectory"). You may wonder if it will be harder to get back in the swing of college if you take time off. Or, you may wonder if colleges prefer a more worldly and experienced student.

Gap years can be meaningful, transformative experiences. If you decide to go that route (and we'll dig in to *how* to decide in a moment), I recommend applying to college as a high school senior and deferring your acceptance once you get in.

The same applies if you anticipate you may need to take a semester or year off before beginning college because of family or health issues—most colleges and universities are willing to work with you to form a path to graduation. Deferred acceptance is available at most colleges (although if you're applying Early Decision or taking advantage of any immediate-decision admission offers, I recommend you confirm that deferral is allowed under those circumstances).

Completing your college application while you're still in school, on a regular schedule and in touch with your teachers, administrators, and high school counselors will be infinitely easier than pulling all of that together after graduation. Plus, knowing where you'll be in a few months or a year will give you peace of mind and allow you to make the most of your semester or year away from school.

How to decide if a gap year is right for you? It comes down to your plan for using the time, the on-campus experience at the colleges you're considering, and the financial impact of taking—and not taking—a year off.

Making a Plan

Most colleges support students who are interested in taking gap years to travel, work, or serve a community. In fact, there is a wide variety of internship, fellowship, and travel programs targeting people in between high school and college. Some colleges even have built-in gap semesters, offering students the chance to spend their first semesters abroad or in an environment outside the classroom. A few examples of gap year activities:

- Serving your community as an AmeriCorp or Service Year Alliance volunteer

- Enrolling in a gap year program through your college (The University of North Carolina offers a year-long global fellowship)

- Working/interning for an organization in your academic or professional area of interest

After you receive your acceptance letter, talk to your college to see if they'll let you start a semester or year later than you had originally planned. Find out what your college needs from you in order to consider your deferment request. Most schools require a formal letter including a description of what you plan to do with your time away from school and, occasionally, a deposit to save your spot. As with most college-related activities, there will be a deadline. Find out what it is before you try to delay your enrollment. Keep in mind: Even if you've already applied for financial aid your senior year, you will need to reapply by completing the FAFSA before you return to school after your gap year. Be sure to ask your college about its financial aid policies for deferred enrollment students.

Financial Considerations

A year without having to pay college tuition might seem like a no-brainer, financially. But, there are actually certain financial advantages to completing your degree as soon as possible. Here's the advice my friend Kal Chany, author of *Paying for College*, gives to those considering a gap year:

- If a large number of students decide to take a gap year, that means a big chunk of students' entry into the workforce will be pushed further into the future. In that case, those who stay the course and graduate sooner will find themselves in a smaller pool of graduates seeking work that requires a college degree—and they will boost both their lifetime earnings potential and their savings by having more time making a premium wage in the workforce before they retire.

- Right now, students and their families have much more leverage in securing larger scholarships and institutional grant aid as colleges are more desperate to maintain enrollment. But in future years, the situation will likely swing back and become more favorable to education providers.

- The rates on federal education loans are extremely low right now as the decline in economic activity due to the pandemic has also resulted in a decline in interest rates. It will likely be cheaper in the long run to borrow *now*, given the fact that all newly originated federal loans have fixed interest rates for the life of the particular loan taken out in a given academic year.

The bottom line? If you have a clear sense of what you want to do with your gap year and a concrete opportunity to pursue it, then deferring college enrollment might be the right choice for you. Once they start their career path, many people find it difficult to take time off to do philanthropy work, immerse themselves in other cultures, travel, or intern in a field they are passionate about, so a gap year can give you that opportunity. Depending on learning styles and thinking patterns, though, it can be difficult for some students to reenter the structure and schedule of university life after a year away. Take plenty of time to reflect and decide what is most important to you. Whatever you decide will be the right choice.

What if I need additional accommodations (and will requesting them hurt my chances of admission)?

Many students need additional accommodations for a variety of reasons, from the dietary to the medical, physical, religious, and academic. Requesting these will **not** hurt your admission chances. Inclusivity has become more than just a buzzword for many colleges; they know that to attract students, they need to provide for *all* students. Legally, if your school accepts any federal financial assistance, it is subject to Section 504 of the Rehabilitation Act of 1973 (which prohibits discrimination), and unless it is a religious institution, it must follow the Americans with Disabilities Act (ADA).

Requesting accommodations is separate from the college application process and usually begins after you have been accepted and enrolled in the college. To save time—especially if there are must-have dealbreakers—you'll want to research these offerings as you look into schools. The easiest way is to do a bit of online research, either on the college's website or through a search engine like Google or Bing. If you're not sure what terms to look for, the most common results will be for "student accessibility services" and your school's name.

Once you've chosen your school, you'll want to contact their disability services department to make your requests. It's a much simpler process than in most high schools, but you'll have to take the first step, as admissions offices are not allowed to request any information about a student's disabilities.

Academic Needs

In the K–12 world, you were likely exposed to IEPs—individual education programs that are covered by the Individuals with Disabilities Education Act. That act doesn't apply to colleges, so there are no IEPs there, and that has some pros and cons. On the positive, this means that if you don't need the accommodations you requested, you can simply stop using them. On the negative, you may not have the same level of support and service. If you need specialized instruction or tutoring, you will have to make sure that option is available *before* you enroll.

Dietary Needs

A growing number of colleges and universities are creating vegetarian, vegan, gluten-free, allergen-friendly, kosher, or halal menus as part of their dining programs. If you have a medical condition that requires certain ingredients (or restricts them), many schools will work to meet them.

Religious Needs

Public schools have a greater legal obligation than do private colleges and universities, but many (from University of Alaska Fairbanks to NYU) will try—even if they don't explicitly state a policy on their website—to accommodate beliefs that may impact your medical, dining, housing, or academic requirements.

Physical Needs

The ADA covers a broad range of diagnoses, including physical disabilities, Autism Spectrum Disorder, ADHD, and speech impairments. Different schools offer different levels of support, but all colleges that get federal funds must ensure equal access to students with disabilities. There is no standard list of accommodations for colleges because everything is considered on an individual basis, but some accommodations are prevalent across institutions. Testing accommodations may include extended time or using a distraction-free room. Note-taking services and audio recording of lectures are also quite common. Other options may include sign language interpreting, accessible desks, flexible attendance, and on-campus housing accommodations.

Keep in mind that although colleges are required to make accommodations for students with disabilities "to a reasonable extent[13]," not all campuses and buildings are outfitted for special accessibility. For example, if you use a wheelchair, examine the campus layout. See where classes are held, how far apart they are, and if there is any inconvenient or undesirable terrain that may impede accessibility for you.

Some universities have well-established disability services departments, which can be a huge plus. If they have worked with students with similar disabilities, they will likely be adept at helping you acquire any necessary accommodations. The most important factor is the school's willingness to

---

[13] https://www2.ed.gov/about/offices/list/ocr/504faq.html

support and work with students with challenges. A motivated institution that communicates well and goes above and beyond can be more valuable than an established but unresponsive disability services department. Talking to or meeting with their staff can be very helpful in narrowing down your college search.

Eleven Stellar Schools for Students With Learning Differences

Marybeth Kravets and Imy Wax, authors of and longtime collabora-tors with us on *The K&W Guide to Colleges for Students with Learning Differences*, have made it their mission to find and profile over 360 schools with programs specifically for students with learning differences. Here are some of the colleges they recommend:

- American University; Washington, DC
- Curry College, Massachusetts
- Lynn University; Florida
- Marist College; New York
- McDaniel College; Maryland
- Mitchell College; Connecticut
- Muskingum College; Ohio
- Northeastern University; Massachusetts
- University of Arizona
- University of Denver; Colorado
- University of the Ozarks; Arkansas

How highly should I weigh a school's stance on social and ethical issues?

That depends on how important the subject is to *you*. How a school holds itself accountable socially, environmentally, and ethically can be hugely important for some people and not a factor at all for others. But if it's important to you, then it should be looked at in the same way that you consider any other factor when deciding what school is a good "cultural fit" (see chapter 1, page 21).

Our annual Colleges Hopes and Worries Survey has shown a notable increase in the importance students place on a school's environmental impact. Our annual Guide to Green Colleges (PrincetonReview.com / college-rankings / green-guide) now features 420 schools, including a list of the top 50. You'll also find that across the board, in addition to traditional public service fields of study and careers, many schools are offering ethically minded studies and programs in everything from social justice to sustainable sciences.

While you can identify your values and their order of importance, it may be challenging to find an exact match when it comes to a school's ethical policies. Due to their magnitude, for however many things they "get right," it is always possible they will do something that doesn't appeal to you. Chances are, if you had to reject every school that wasn't 100% in line with your goals, you'd probably have to reject *every* school.

What you can do, then, is be *aware*. You can assess whether a school's current practices, policies, and programs align with your values, and if they don't, you should explore other options. Your actual coursework will likely be challenging enough without having to also cope with the dissonance that comes from feeling that your tuition is actively causing harm.

One strategy is to find a compromise without compromising your values. If, for instance, you were opposed to non-fungible tokens (NFTs) and learned that your school was attempting to fundraise by creating content on the blockchain, you wouldn't have to tear up your application or switch colleges. Instead, you might take that as an opportunity to work from within the school to push back against that policy, to educate classmates and faculty alike. Alternatively, if you were concerned about your meal plan dollars going toward non-sustainable food sources, you might look to start a fund that could offset that money by giving equally to local farms and businesses, similarly to how people seek to offset their carbon footprint.

Ultimately, instead of thinking about how highly to weigh your *school's* ethical responsibilities, look at your own, and let your values help steer you toward the college that will be your best fit, where you can both be most impacted and make the most impact.

What impact will cheaters have on my admissions chances?

When the college admissions bribery scandal broke in 2019, I started getting a lot of questions about how those who were cheating the system would impact their (or their child's) chances. Students with the financial means to attend independent schools already have outsized chances to get into elite schools like Princeton and Yale; 98% of all students attend public school, yet over 20% of the student body at these elite institutions comes from private high schools.

Repugnant as it may be that some parents attempted to buy their students admission, I encourage you to look at the overwhelming majority of admissions, which are based on academic records and increasingly detailed (and sometimes holistic) assessment tools. Some three million students apply, fair and square, to colleges each year. Worrying about the rare individuals who are attempting to cheat the system won't help your application. Rather than stressing over the opportunities other students might have, dedicate yourself to emphasizing the unique background that makes you, *you.*

Focus on taking challenging classes, getting good grades, achieving high test scores, and participating in activities that demonstrate your sincere passions and interests. Colleges want to see what you really care about and how and where you devote your time. Think less about being "well rounded" and more about showcasing your unique interests. You don't need to be class president, captain of the debate team, or a coder extraordinaire to be a great candidate. Also, it never hurts to show schools that you're interested in them. Visit, take a tour, sit in on a class, schedule an interview, and reach out with questions; be more than just a name on an application.

Character Counts

To get a better reflection of the student beyond their test scores and grades, some schools, including Bucknell University, MIT, and Swarthmore College, are examining alternative assessment tools to measure an applicant's character attributes. "We are not saying throw out testing and replace it with noncognitive measures," said William T. Conley, the vice president for enrollment management at Bucknell. "But we know that things like persistence and teamwork are important to success in college and afterward, and they should be part of holistic admissions[14]."

[14] theatlantic.com/education/archive/2019/03/college-admissions-scandals-are-impossible-prevent/585361/

How can a parent participate most effectively in their child's college application process?

I love this question. Parents, I know the college admission process can be a stressful one for you, too. Family members can be the biggest cheerleaders for the kids in their lives going through the process, but they often don't know *how* or *how much* to be involved. Sometimes parents hold back because they feel shaky themselves on the admission process or feel that applying to college is an important rite of passage that students should do all on their own. Other parents feel their best role is to act as hand-holder or drill sergeant, putting their kids through their college application paces.

> Family members can be a huge support to the students in their life by offering both moral and logistical support.

Folks, there is a happy medium! Parents and other family members can be a huge support to the students in their lives by offering both moral and logistical support in tackling that long list of college application tasks. Help them get organized and break the tasks into bite-sized pieces with a planner, such as *The Complete College Planner*. Build up morale by offering to take your applicant on college tours and to visit college fairs. Help them research and compare colleges. Ask lots of questions! With new health and safety protocols at college campuses nationwide, you'll want to make sure the coronavirus response for the schools on your child's list is one you both feel comfortable with.

When it comes to college conversations, my six biggest tips are:

1. **Set some ground rules.** This might seem like a no brainer, but it's extremely important for parents to get their own college worries in check before broaching these weighty topics with students. You want conversations with your child to be positive and productive. Don't pass your stress along to your students because they may not want to open up to you later when they hit an application snag. Your kids are going to take their cues from you about how to approach the college admission process. Remember you're on stage all the time. You don't have to be perfect, but when you sense yourself losing your perspective, revert back to setting good examples.

2. **Start early.** This is the MOST popular piece of advice given by parents who have gone through the process. (About 50% of respondents to our annual Colleges Hopes & Worries Survey say this). Refer back to Chapter 3, where I outline exactly what students should be doing in 9th, 10th, 11th, and 12th grades to prepare for the college admission process. I've said it before, folks, but planning ahead won't just set your child up to succeed, it will actually make the process so much less stressful. (More about stress, later!)

3. **Help students find balance.** It's possible to be too focused on getting into college. Of course, we all want our children and students to care about their futures. But if they make every decision in high school based on how it will look to colleges, they're trying to game the system rather than follow their own interests. That never works in college admissions, and it doesn't make for a happy, confident kid, either. So, don't tie everything students do to college. Help them find a balance between college planning and the other parts of their lives. They'll be more content and more successful college applicants if you do. (Pro tip: Implement a "college-free" talk zone at the dinner table or on the ride home from school so your kids can get a break from college overload!)

4. **Create a rock-solid support system.** There's a reason you don't ask your doctor to do your taxes or your accountant to diagnose your knee pain. Go to the right sources. Your child's high school counselor, college websites, college guidebooks, admission officers, representatives at virtual information sessions, and students who attend the schools are good sources.

5. **Help your child figure out the kind of college atmosphere in which they'll thrive academically, personally, socially, and, yes, financially.** This all goes back to "best-fit colleges," which I discuss back in Chapter 1. It's not all about where your child can get in, where you, the parent, went to college, or the college with the best name recognition. You're looking for the schools that will fit your student to a T. You know your child best (and probably feel you know best about where they would thrive), but be patient with your child as they work through the journey. Communicate your opinions but be open to negotiating with your student and to compromise. That being said, do talk about finances and college costs early on, and make sure a financial safety school (one your child would be thrilled to attend) makes it on their list.

6. **Ask your student: "What's the best way for me to help you?"** Parents who deliver meticulously organized file folders with college lists and typed up college essays to their teen's door are likely to be met with more than a few eye rolls. (It goes without saying that parents should NEVER write their child's essays or fill out their applications for them). Let your child take the reins on certain pieces of the process and slowly gain more and more responsibility. This is the first major project your child is going to undertake with no final grade and no teacher leading the way! Your role is to help them to strategize, divide, and conquer.

That's my advice for parents. But what about advice for students? Lean on your parents when you need to, but don't let them make all the decisions!

Parent to Parent: 8 Tips Parents of College-Bound Students Need to Know

1. "Listen to your child!—Maureen, Middletown, NY

2. "Allow your child to dream about anything they can be!" —Susan, Remsenburg, NJ

3. "Be a guide and not a choice-maker. Believe in your child's own intuitions and advocate for their personal interests." —Alice, Randolph, NJ

4. "As a parent, allow your kid to experience the college application for themselves. While it is imperative to gently look over their shoulders, taking over full control doesn't allow them to make important decisions for themselves." —Danielle, Lambertville, NJ

5. "Be encouraging but not micromanaging. Remind your child of upcoming deadlines and help them proofread their essays. Start early in researching colleges that might be a good fit. Help your child pick out a good review manual for the ACT and/or SAT." —Carole, Livonia, MI

6. "I know some parents who are literally obsessing over this whole process. I hope they don't forget that it is their child that is going to college, not them." —Nancy, WI

7. "Focus on your child and what is best for them and try not to focus on all the competition between parents. This is about your child, not about you." —Carol, Tarrytown, NY

8. "Parents, back off! Applicants, relax!" —D.B., Monterey, CA

—College Hopes & Worries Survey

How do I balance schoolwork, extracurriculars, test prep, college applications, family, social life, and SANITY?!

In the words of one recent college applicant who completed our annual College Hopes & Worries Survey: "Whoever said that senior year is the easiest is a liar."

I do not envy the schedule of today's high school students one bit. As they juggle homework, family life, and extracurriculars, all amidst a global pandemic, college-bound students are facing very serious pressures, not the least of which is the overwhelming terrain of the college admission process.

Just know that you are not alone. I hope that this book has done some good in diffusing the perceived enormity of the process and has reassured you that the college admissions process is actually a very exciting time in your life and not one to be feared. Now that you understand the timeline and have a sense of the steps you need to accomplish, take a deep breath and dig in.

> "It's easier to break a boulder into pieces than to try to move it all at once."

First, it's important to get organized. Make a college checklist of all the things you need to do for your applications. (We've got a great one in the Appendix.) From asking teachers for college recommendations to applying for financial aid and scholarships, assign yourself deadlines and put them all on the list. Then, plot your application-related deadlines in a notebook or calendar app along with your homework, projects, and papers. Don't forget to schedule time on the calendar for your away games or work shifts. The goal is to map out everything you must accomplish over the month, semester, or year.

Not only does this system ensure that nothing falls through the cracks, but plotting your schedule will help you see your pressure points. Do you have a college application deadline and a major chem final on the same day? Avoid a head-on collision by getting your application done early! Remember, you can't necessarily study too far in advance, but you can work on your applications whenever you have some down time—like drafting those college essays over spring or summer break.

Ok, you've laid out all your to-dos in a big old grid/worksheet/calendar. Now what? Take things one step at a time. Break your big projects into little ones. It's easier to plan, and every task you get done will help you feel more confident and accomplished. As one college counselor I know puts it, "It's easier to break a boulder into pieces than to try to move it all at once."

Remember: You have a support system. Your friends, your parents, and your college counselors are all in your corner. Just talking with others can be a source of help, as well as a way to relieve some of the stress of becoming too wrapped up in your own situation. Take advantage of workshops your school's counseling office may offer on specific aspects of the admission process. At The Princeton Review, our YouTube channel is packed with playlists just for you on many college admission topics from financial aid and writing a great college essay to the latest SAT, ACT, and AP exam updates. (Check them out at YouTube.com/ThePrincetonReview.)

The bottom line on stress? Though there isn't much that students can do to get the colleges to make their decisions any faster, there are some strategies to prevent the worst stress. If you ask lots of questions to help you understand the process, start early, take it one step at a time, and apply to several carefully selected, appropriate schools, you can rest assured that you've done everything in your power to make the process go as smoothly as possible.

5 Things a College Counselor Can Do for You

1. **Lower your college stress.** Applications are stressful, but knowing that there are college experts on your side can make all the difference.

2. **Make a college wish list.** Talking to your counselor about your dreams and what's important to you in academics, campus life, and financial aid will help you figure out what you really want out of college.

3. **Find and compare colleges.** College counselors are pros at helping you research the schools that are the right fit for your unique personality and goals.

4. **Help you rise to the top.** Your college counselor will help you position the rest of your application to tell your story through your essays, extracurricular activities, and letters of recommendation.

5. **Choose the right school for you.** Your counselor will help you craft your list of dream, match, and safety schools, and create the right application strategy for your college wish list.

Appendix

College-Bound: Your Admission Checklist 213

High School Testing Timeline...215

26 Tips for Getting Financial Aid, Scholarships, and Grants and For
    Paying Less for College..216

More Advice from the Experts: Smart Tips from College-Bound
    Students for Next Year's Applicants 219

Parent to Parent: What I Wish I'd Known...222

Here's Another Helpful Resource

The college profiles on The Princeton Review's website contain meticulously researched information that will help you narrow the search for the best college for you. Browse user-friendly profiles and get answers to your questions about tuition and other costs, average test scores, popular majors, student housing, and key campus organizations at PrincetonReview.com/college-search.

Find out more about kicking off your college search in Chapter 1.

College Bound: Your Admission Checklist

What's the trick to less college admission stress? Start early, and take small steps along the way.

Freshman Year

- ☐ Focus on your grades so you can earn placement for more rigorous courses.

- ☐ Practice your study skills, identify support resources available, and ask for help if you need it.

- ☐ Get to know your school and community! Explore clubs, sports, volunteer opportunities, and more.

Sophomore Year

- ☐ Continue to challenge yourself academically.

- ☐ Develop constructive relationships with your teachers.

- ☐ Get to know your school counselor.

- ☐ Commit to the activities that you really enjoy, and try to take on more responsibility.

Summer Before Junior Year

- ☐ This is the perfect time to prep for the SAT and ACT.

- ☐ Begin your college research.

Junior Year

- ☐ Take the SAT and ACT when you're ready.

- ☐ Balance schoolwork and outside-school interests.

- ☐ Take the most challenging courses available to you.

- ☐ Take the PSAT/NMSQT in October to qualify for a National Merit Scholarship and other scholarship opportunities.

- ☐ Start gathering teacher recommendations.

- ☐ Narrow your college list and try to visit one or two campuses, if it's possible to do so. Virtual college tours and online information sessions are your friends!

☐ Make a plan to prepare for AP exams in May.

☐ Learn about financial aid and available scholarships.

Summer Before Senior Year

☐ Start working on your application and prewriting college essays—they take longer than you think!

☐ Make a calendar of all your application deadlines so you can stay on track.

☐ If possible, consider visiting colleges that have made it to the top of your target list.

☐ If you are applying for Early Decision, you should take the SAT or ACT no later than September.

Senior Fall

☐ Apply early if you're a strong candidate.

☐ Wrap up your applications and stay on top of deadlines for apps, scholarships, and financial aid.

☐ Don't get senioritis! Senior grades matter—your first term grades will definitely be used in the admission process.

☐ Complete your last SAT/ACT by December at the latest.

Senior Spring

☐ If you still have AP exams to take, study!

☐ Send thank-you notes to your recommenders.

☐ Get ready to celebrate! Spring is all about acceptance letters rolling in.

☐ Talk to friends, family, and counselors before making your final choice.

☐ Once you decide, don't look back! Read through your college's course catalog, and look forward to the next four years.

High School Testing Timeline

Extracurricular activities, school commitments, and other factors play into when and how you're going to prepare for the SAT and ACT.

If you're taking both tests, you need to leave enough time to take each test twice. It's ideal for students to prep for the SAT over the summer and take the PSAT in October. You'll be ready for the PSAT because you will have already prepared for the SAT.

Folks, there's no perfect plan. Here's what I recommend for students going into their junior year.

Prep for the SAT and ACT, and AP Exams

- ☐ **Summer before junior year:** Prep for the SAT and take it in August or October for the first time.

- ☐ **October:** Take the PSAT.

- ☐ **November/December:** Take the SAT one more time.

- ☐ **February:** Start prepping for the ACT and take it for the first time.

- ☐ **April:** Take the ACT one more time.

- ☐ **May:** Study, and take your AP tests.

- ☐ **Summer before senior year:** You can take the SAT or ACT one more time if necessary. If you take a summer test, you receive scores in time for Early Action or Early Decision deadlines.

26 Tips for Getting Financial Aid, Scholarships, and Grants and for Paying Less for College

When it comes to actually paying for college, there is a lot of information out there. As I have mentioned, a great resource is our annual book *Paying for College* by my friend Kalman Chany. Here, I present some tips from Kal for applying for financial aid and trimming the costs of college.

Getting Financial Aid

1. **Learn how financial aid works.** The more and the sooner you know about how need-based aid eligibility is determined, the better you can take steps to maximize such eligibility.

2. **Apply for financial aid no matter what your circumstances.** Some merit-based aid can only be awarded if the applicant has submitted financial aid application forms.

3. **Don't wait until the student is accepted to apply for financial aid.** Do it when applying for admission.

4. **Complete all the required aid applications.** All students seeking aid must submit the FAFSA (Free Application for Federal Student Aid); other forms may also be required. Check with each college to see what's required and when.

5. **Get the best scores you can on the SAT or ACT.** They are used not only in decisions for admission but they can also impact financial aid. If your scores and other stats exceed the school's admission criteria, you are likely to get a better aid package than a marginal applicant.

6. **Apply strategically to colleges.** Your chances of getting aid will be better at schools that have generous financial aid budgets. (Check the Financial Aid Ratings for various schools on PrincetonReview.com.)

7. **Don't rule out any school as too expensive.** A generous aid award from a pricey private school can make it less costly than a public school with a lower sticker price.

8. **Take advantage of education tax benefits.** A dollar saved on taxes is worth the same as a dollar in scholarship aid. Look into Coverdells, 529 Plans, education tax credits, and loan deductions.

Scholarships and Grants

9. **Get your best possible score on the PSAT:** It is the National Merit Scholarship Qualifying Test and also used in the selection of students for other scholarships and recognition programs.

10. **Check your eligibility for grants and scholarships from your state.** Some (but not all) states will allow you to use such funds out of state.

11. **Look for scholarships locally.** Find out if your employer offers scholarships or tuition assistance plans for employees or family members. Also look into scholarships from your community groups and high school, as well as your church, temple, or mosque.

12. **Look for outside scholarships realistically:** they account for less than 5% of aid awarded. Research them at PrincetonReview.com or other free sites. Steer clear of scholarship search firms that charge fees and "promise" scholarships.

Paying for College

13. **Start saving early when the student is an infant.** Too late? Start now. The more you save, the less you'll have to borrow.

14. **Invest wisely.** Considering a 529 plan? Compare your own state's plan which may have tax benefits with other states' programs. Get info at https://www.savingforcollege.com/.

15. **If you have to borrow, first pursue federal education loans (Direct or PLUS).** Avoid private loans at all costs.

16. **Never put tuition on a credit card.** The debt is more expensive than ever given recent changes to interest rates and other fees some card issuers are now charging.

17. **Try not to take money from a retirement account or 401(k) to pay for college.** In addition to likely early distribution penalties and additional income taxes, the higher income will reduce your aid eligibility.

Paying Less for College

18. **Attend a community college for two years and transfer to a pricier school to complete the degree.** Plan ahead: Be sure the college you plan to transfer to will accept the community college credits.

19. **Look into "cooperative education" programs.** Over 900 colleges allow students to combine college education with a job. It can take longer to complete a degree this way. But graduates generally owe less in student loans and have a better chance of getting hired.

20. **Take as many AP courses as possible and get high scores on AP exams.** Many colleges award course credits for high AP scores. Some students have cut a year off their college tuition this way.

21. **Earn college credit via "dual enrollment" programs available at some high schools.** These allow students to take college level courses during their senior year.

22. **Earn college credits by taking CLEP (College-Level Examination Program) exams.** Depending on the college, a qualifying score on any of the thirty-three CLEP exams can earn students three to twelve college credits.

23. **Stick to your college and your major.** Changing colleges can result in lost credits. Aid may be limited/not available for transfer students at some schools. Changing majors can mean paying for extra courses to meet requirements.

24. **Finish college in three years if possible.** Take the maximum number of credits every semester, attend summer sessions, and earn credits via online courses. Some colleges offer three-year programs for high-achieving students.

25. **Let Uncle Sam pay for your degree.** ROTC (Reserve Officer Training Corps) programs available from U.S. Armed Forces branches (except the Coast Guard) offer merit-based scholarships up to full tuition via participating colleges in exchange for military service after you graduate.

26. **Better yet:** Attend a tuition-free college.

Please visit PrincetonReview.com/college-advice for the most up-to-date information on available financial aid programs.

More Advice from the Experts: Smart Tips from College-Bound Students for Next Year's Applicants

Every year on our College Hopes & Worries Survey, we include an optional question at the end that asks respondents what advice they have for next year's applicants and parents of applicants. Here, in their own words, are the suggestions and tips of our respondents. Enjoy!

On the College Application Process

"Start early. As a matter of fact, start now."

"Two Words: Start Early! Deadlines creep up quicker than you may anticipate. In addition, there are little things that you need to do to fulfill the application requirements. By starting early you can reduce stress levels and assure that you have enough time to get everything finished without rushing."

"Research, research, research. The better educated you are about the colleges, the better chance you will get the education you really want."

"Be excited to write your college application essays. They WILL definitely be tough, but in the end, you'll look back at the experience and smile because you learn so much about yourself as a human being. It's actually quite a wonderful experience, but only if you're willing to make it a wonderful experience."

"Make sure that you apply or consider all the schools that you could possibly conceive yourself going to. Nothing is worse than 'February syndrome' in which you realize you didn't apply to a school that you could see yourself attending."

On Stress

"College is about finding your happiness, not your parents' happiness or what would look good on your bumper. Be open-minded."

"Don't get frustrated with applications. Just think of how good you'll feel in the fall walking the halls of your chosen college."

"Have fun with it! If you enjoy the process along the way, the outcome will hopefully be more beneficial."

"Do not get too nervous. It's not always about getting into the most known school."

"Don't worry! It's going to be okay."

On Money Matters

"Don't let the cost of a college scare you. Apply anyways because financial aid is always available."

"Money is a huge factor for both you and your child. It is extremely important that you give your child a 'budget' for your peace of mind and theirs."

"Scholarships! Make sure you apply for as many scholarships as possible."

"Don't give up, apply to your dream school even if you can't afford it, you might be surprised by how much financial aid is offered."

"More expensive colleges are not always better colleges."

On Rejection

"When you think you didn't get into the school you wanted, you might be getting into the school you needed."

"You are smart. Don't let a rejection letter make you feel depressed."

"There is a place for everyone. Relax and think of it as a journey—not a race to be won, but a home to be found."

"It's not as bad as everyone makes it out to be. Don't worry so much about where you're going. Worry more about the mindset you go to school with."

"Try not to stress too much about the possibility of not being accepted into your first-choice college, because you'll go half mad if you do so."

On Choosing Which College to Attend

"Don't worry so much about what other people think is the best college for you. The only opinion that matters is your own because you will be the one spending four years of your life there. Pick the college you feel most comfortable at."

"Learn as much as you can about the college application process. Things have changed so much from the time my parents went through this."

"Don't rule out schools just because they aren't Ivy League caliber. Smaller schools have a lot to offer."

"Don't focus on your first choice. Widen your eyes to keep your options open."

Here's Another Helpful Book

My book *Colleges That Create Futures: 50 Schools That Launch Careers By Going Beyond the Classroom* salutes an extraordinary group of institutions with compelling commitments to helping students segue to successful careers and post-graduate accomplishments.

Check out a sampling of noteworthy campus experiences in Chapter 1.

Parent to Parent: What I Wish I'd Known

Every year on our College Hopes & Worries Survey, we include an optional question at the end that asks respondents what advice they have for next year's applicants and parents of applicants. Here's what the parents had to say.

On the College Application Process

"Start sooner!" —Linda, Tampa FL

"Start early, and save early for their future." —Loreli, Chandler, AZ

"Start early! Visit schools in sophomore year, concentrate on testing in junior year, apply in senior year." —Karen, Woodinville, WA

"Start preparing in your child's first year of high school. Don't wait until third year." —Carlene, Roseville, CA

"Start the whole process a year earlier than you think you need to." —Amy, Glen Ellyn, IL

"When thinking about which schools to consider, our daughter seemed stuck because she isn't sure what she wants to be. We tried to help her just think about three to five things she likes and would want to learn more about. That seemed to help take off the pressure and get her 'unstuck' with choosing some schools to visit." —Ellen, New Paltz, NY

"Create a calendar with deadlines, test dates, college events and visits, etc. This will eliminate a lot of stress for you and your child." —Sandee, Los Gatos, CA

"Treat the application process like a job. Set a regular time each week to tackle some aspect of the process." —Laura, ME

"After your child applies, the schools will allow you access to their website to track your application information. Keep track of all of your child's passwords and website access information. Because schools use different safety systems, you can end up with different user IDs and passwords at each school. If you apply to more than three schools, this can be quite confusing." —Cheryl, Stevenson Ranch, CA

"Do what you can to make sure your child 'owns' the entire application process. Start the FAFSA and CSS early as they require a lot of information and pay careful attention to the instructions. Don't wait until the last day to apply for anything as the servers frequently get overloaded." —James, CA

On Stress

"Relax! Somehow, it all comes together. Everyone goes through it, so ask your family and friends for advice/help. You will be surprised at the great advice you can gather that way." —Sharon, Brielle, NJ

"Your child will not be nearly as stressed as you will be." —Lynda, Sunrise, FL

"Don't spend too much time comparing notes with others going through the process. Makes people crazy." —Sarah, Newton, MA

"Try not to stress too much—enjoy the process and make the most of the time you spend with your child, talking about their interests, helping them take that big step." —Sharon, Amherst, MA

"Make sure to take the college process in steps and you won't feel so overwhelmed." —Denise, Sea Girt, NJ

On Parenting

"Listen to your child!" —Maureen, Middletown, NY

"Allow your child to dream about anything they can be!" —Susan, NJ

"Be a guide and not a choice-maker. Believe in your child's own intuitions and advocate for their personal interests." —Alice, Randolph, NJ

"As a parent, allow your kid to experience the college application for themselves. While it is imperative to gently look over their shoulders, taking over full control doesn't allow them to make important decisions for themselves." —Danielle, Lambertville, NJ

"I know some parents who are literally obsessing over this whole process. I hope they don't forget that it is their child that is going to college, not them." —Nancy, WI

On Money Matters

"Look at the average financial aid package, not just cost, and don't say no to yourself (your child) on behalf of a school by never applying to it." —Charles, Philadelphia, PA

"Dare to dream. Don't limit your child's vision of their future by your own financial worries." —Karen, VA

"Don't be scared off from applying to private schools as opposed to public universities. Private schools can be very generous with scholarship offers." —Diane, Chicago IL

"Let your child be free to see what schools will accept your child and see what the financials are later. In other words, do not assume a school is too much money as a reason not to apply. Particularly if your child has done well on ACT/SAT, the tuition number at a private school is not going to be the number you will have to fund." —Alan, MI

"Do your homework on the entire process, including understanding how the financial aid process works, and don't wait until the last minute to delve into this stuff." —Ken, Colorado Springs, CO

On Choosing Which College to Attend

"Let your student take the lead in defining interests and schools that could be a good fit. Don't focus on labels. An excellent education can be had in schools you've never heard about before." —C.L., Ridgewood, NJ

"Don't be overly focused on 'brand name' colleges. There are other excellent choices that offer very good value, and are quite affordable." —Mark, Macungie, PA

"Don't focus on a major so much as interests and opportunities. Nobody is sure at 18 what they want to do. The beauty of college is you have a chance to expand your horizons and perspective." —Larry, Bayside, NY

"There are many good colleges out there—not just the ten that everyone is applying to." —M.M., Far Hills, NJ

"Make the final decision after receiving all the financial aid packages." —Kathleen, FL

Here's Another Helpful Book

The K&W Guide to Colleges for Students with Learning Differences profiles over 360 schools highly recommended for such students. It includes strategies to help them successfully apply to the best programs for their needs, plus advice from learning specialists on making an effective transition to college.

NOTES